STAAR Mathematics

PRACTICE

M000107086

30126000226065

Table of Contents

Forest Creek ES
Library

Using This Book

What Is the STAAR Mathematics Assessment?

The State of Texas Assessments of Academic Readiness (STAAR) is the current assessment for students in the state of Texas. STAAR Mathematics assesses what students are expected to learn at each grade level according to the developmentally appropriate academic readiness and supporting standards outlined in the Texas Essential Knowledge and Skills (TEKS).

How Does This Book Help My Student(s)?

If your student is taking the STAAR Assessment for Mathematics, then as a teacher and/or parent you can use the mini-lessons, math practice pages and practice tests in this book to prepare for the STAAR Mathematics exam. This book is appropriate for on-grade-level students.

STAAR Mathematics Practice provides:

- Mini-lessons for assessed Math TEKS skills and strategies
- Word problems for assessed Math TEKS skills and strategies
- Questions for griddable and multiple-choice answer format
- Opportunities to familiarize students with STAAR format and question stems

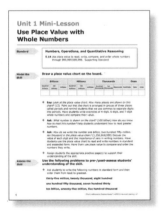

Introduce STAAR-aligned math concept, skill, or strategy

Practice with STAAR-aligned problems

Assess concepts, skills, and strategies with word problems

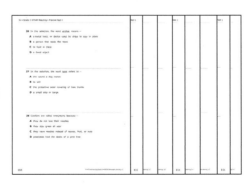

Simulate test-taking with full-length practice tests

STAAR Mathematics Practice/Assessed TEKS Alignment Chart • Grade 5

I. Number, Operations, and Quantitative Reasoning	5.1	5.2	5.3	5.4	5.5	5.6	5.7	5.8	5.9	5.10	5.11	5.12	5.13	5.14–5.16
Unit 1: Use Place Value with Whole Numbers	✔													✔
Unit 2: Use Place Value with Decimals	✔													✔
Unit 3: Compare and Order Decimals	✔													✔
Unit 4: Add and Subtract Whole Numbers			✔											✔
Unit 5: Add and Subtract Decimals			✔											✔
Unit 6: Identify Factors and Multiples			✔											✔
Unit 7: Multiply Whole Numbers			✔											✔
Unit 8: Divide by a One-Digit Divisor			✔											✔
Unit 9: Divide by a Two-Digit Divisor			✔											✔
Unit 10: Estimate Solutions				✔										✔
Unit 11: Relate Decimals to Fractions		✔												✔
Unit 12: Find Equivalent Fractions		✔												✔
Unit 13: Generate Mixed Numbers and Improper Fractions		✔												✔
Unit 14: Compare Fractions to Solve Problems		✔												✔
Unit 15: Add and Subtract Fractions			✔											✔

II. Patterns, Relationships, and Algebraic Reasoning	5.1	5.2	5.3	5.4	5.5	5.6	5.7	5.8	5.9	5.10	5.11	5.12	5.13	5.14–5.16
Unit 16: Describe Relationships					✔									✔
Unit 17: Identify Prime and Composite Numbers					✔									✔
Unit 18: Write Equations						✔								✔

III. Geometry and Spatial Reasoning	5.1	5.2	5.3	5.4	5.5	5.6	5.7	5.8	5.9	5.10	5.11	5.12	5.13	5.14–5.16
Unit 19: Classify Quadrilaterals							✔							✔
Unit 20: Classify Geometric Figures							✔							✔
Unit 21: Locate Points on the Coordinate Plane									✔					✔
Unit 22: Identify Transformations								✔						✔

IV. Measurement	5.1	5.2	5.3	5.4	5.5	5.6	5.7	5.8	5.9	5.10	5.11	5.12	5.13	5.14–5.16
Unit 23: Convert Among Metric Units										✔				✔
Unit 24: Convert Among Customary Units										✔				✔
Unit 25: Find Perimeter and Area										✔				✔
Unit 26: Find Volume										✔				✔
Unit 27: Solve Problems with Temperature and Time											✔			✔

V. Probability and Statistics	5.1	5.2	5.3	5.4	5.5	5.6	5.7	5.8	5.9	5.10	5.11	5.12	5.13	5.14–5.16
Unit 28: Conduct Probability Experiments												✔		✔
Unit 29: Make Predictions												✔		✔
Unit 30: Make Line Graphs from Tables													✔	✔
Unit 31: Find Median, Mode, and Range													✔	✔
Unit 32: Graph Data													✔	✔

Unit 1 Mini-Lesson
Use Place Value with Whole Numbers

Standard

Number, Operations, and Quantitative Reasoning

5.1A (SS) Use place value to read, write, compare, and order whole numbers through 999,999,999,999.

Model the Skill

Draw a place value chart on the board.

Billions			Millions			Thousands			Ones		
hundred billions	ten billions	billions	hundred millions	ten millions	millions	hundred thousands	ten thousands	thousands	hundreds	tens	ones
1	0	0,	0	0	0,	0	0	0,	0	0	0

◆ **Say:** *Look at the place value chart. How many places are shown on this chart?* (12) Point out that the chart is arranged in groups of three places called periods and remind students that we use commas to separate digits into periods. Have students write examples of 4-digit, 6-digit, and 7-digit whole numbers and compare their value.

◆ **Ask:** *What number is shown on the chart?* (100 billion) *How do you know how to read this number?* Help students understand how to read greater numbers.

◆ **Ask:** *How do we write the number one billion, two hundred fifty million, ten thousand in the place value chart?* (1,250,010,000) Discuss the value of each digit and the importance of zero in writing numbers. Have students use the place value chart to read and write numbers in standard and expanded form. Have them use place value to compare and order the numbers they write.

◆ Assign students the appropriate practice page(s) to support their understanding of the skill.

Assess the Skill

Use the following problems to pre-/post-assess students' understanding of the skill.

◆ Ask students to write the following numbers in standard form and then order them from least to greatest.

thirty-five million, twenty thousand, eight hundred

one hundred fifty thousand, seven hundred thirty

ten billion, seventy-five million, five hundred thousand

Name _____ **Date** _____

Write or compare numbers as indicated. Use the place value chart to help you.

Billions			Millions			Thousands			Ones			
hundred billions	ten billions	billions	hundred millions	ten millions	millions	hundred thousands	ten thousands	thousands	hundreds	tens	ones

1 one hundred fifty thousand, six hundred three

standard form: _____

2 one billion, two million, three thousand

standard form: _____

3 15,302,750

written form: _____

4 105,406

expanded form: _____ + _____ + _____ + _____

5 100,783 ◯ 10,078

6 9,674 ◯ 9,673

7 5,400,860 ◯ 50,408,600

8 27,836 ◯ 27,825

9 1,000,900,500 ◯ 1,000,900,500

10 1,234,506 ◯ 123,400,506

| > is greater than |
| < is less than |
| = is equal to |

☆ **Tell how place value helps you compare two numbers.**

Name _____ Date _____

Write each number as indicated.

1 standard form: 10,875
expanded form: 10,000 + 800 + 70 + 5
written form: _____

2 standard form: 105,250
expanded form: _____
written form: _____

3 standard form: _____
expanded form: _____
written form: four million thirty thousand nine hundred fifty-seven

4 standard form: _____
expanded form: 10,000,000 + 700,000 + 5,000 + 800 + 90 + 1
written form: _____

Compare the numbers in the box. Use >, <, or =.

5 _____ ◯ _____

6 _____ ◯ _____

7 _____ ◯ _____

8 _____ ◯ _____

9 _____ ◯ _____

408,083
380,746
81,740
501,004
101,978

10 The numbers in order from least to greatest are _____

 Tell the steps you took to write the numbers in order.

Name _____ Date _____

Solve.

1 Write the following number in written form.

10,003,459,027

_____

_____

2 Write the following number in standard form.

four hundred one million seven hundred two thousand three hundred sixty-eight

_____

3 Write the following number in expanded form.

42,060,839

_____

_____

4 Use symbols to show the relationship between the following three numbers.

12,111,320   8,979,554   9,461,008

_____

Circle the letter for the correct answer.

5 Which number is greater than 672,199,023 and less than 726,098,400?

A 707,555,399

B 669,087,999

C 742,058,372

D 67,900,000

6 Which is the standard representation of five billion, sixty million, eleven thousand twelve?

A 5,061,100,012

B 5,560,110,012

C 5,060,110,012

D 5,060,011,012

7 The table below shows the number of hamburgers sold each year.

Restaurant	Number of Burgers Sold
Amy's	1,246,780
Best Burger	1,262,000
Burger Empire	875,925

Based on this information, which of the following statements is true?

A Amy's sold the greatest number of burgers.

B Best Burger sold the least number of burgers.

C Burger Empire sold the most burgers.

D Best Burger sold the most burgers.

Unit 2 Mini-Lesson ★
Use Place Value with Decimals

Standard

Number, Operations, and Quantitative Reasoning

5.1B (SS) Use place value to read, write, compare, and order decimals through the thousandths place.

Model the Skill

Draw a place value chart on the board.

hundreds	tens	ones	.	tenths	hundredths	thousandths
			.			

◆ **Say:** *Look at the place value chart. How many places are shown on this chart?* (6) *Which place is the greatest?* (hundreds) Point out the decimal point and explain that three places are to the left of the decimal point and three places are to the right of the decimal point.

◆ **Ask:** *How does the tens place compare to the ones place?* (The tens place is 10 times more than the ones place.) Explain that each place is 1/10 of the place to its left—the tenths place is 1/10 of the ones place. Have students write the number "one hundred four and thirty-eight hundredths" in the place value chart. Point out that **and** indicates there is a fraction of a number, or a decimal amount, that follows the whole number portion.

◆ **Ask:** *How do we write one hundred four in the place value chart?* (1 in the hundreds, 0 in the tens, and 4 in the ones) *How do we write thirty-eight hundredths in the place value chart?* (3 in the tenths place, 8 in the hundredths place) Demonstrate how to use the numbers written in the chart to write the standard form. (104.38) Have students look at the standard form and say the number aloud, making sure that it matches the word form.

◆ Assign students the appropriate practice page(s) to support their understanding of the skill.

Assess the Skill

Use the following problems to pre-/post-assess students' understanding of the skill.

◆ Ask students to write the following decimals in standard, expanded, and written form:
  • sixty-five and eight hundredths
  • one hundred thirty and forty-four hundredths
  • five hundred one and eighty-six thousandths

Name _____ Date _____

Read each number. Write its word name. Use the place value chart to help you.

hundreds	tens	ones	.	tenths	hundredths	thousandths
			.			

1 standard form: 24.76

expanded form: _____

written form: _____

2 standard form: 21.035

expanded form: _____

written form: _____

3 standard form: 400.04

expanded form: _____

written form: _____

4 standard form: 121.06

expanded form: _____

written form: _____

5 standard form: _____

expanded form: _____

written form: three hundred five and five-tenths

6 standard form: _____

expanded form: _____

written form: seven hundred eighteen and twelve-thousandths

7 standard form: _____

expanded form: $90 + 9 + \frac{8}{10} + \frac{3}{100}$

written form: _____

8 standard form: 300.4

expanded form: _____

written form: _____

 Tell how place value helps you read and write a number.

Name _____ Date _____

Complete the chart.

	Standard Form	Expanded Form	Written Form
❶	6.17		
❷		$30 + 5 + \frac{2}{10}$	
❸		$4 + \frac{5}{10} + \frac{7}{100} + \frac{9}{1,000}$	
❹			eight hundred two and six-hundredths
❺	206.047		
❻	74.21		
❼	8.096		
❽			twenty and sixty–two hundredths
❾			ninety-five and four-tenths
❿		$600 + 5 + \frac{3}{100}$	

 Tell how you know the value of each digit in a number.

Name _____ Date _____

Solve.

1 Write 510.401 in expanded form.

2 Write three hundred fifty-two and four-tenths in standard form.

3 Write 10.7 in written form.

4 Write seven hundred one and one-thousandth in standard form.

5 Write $200 + 50 + 7 + \frac{5}{10} + \frac{7}{100} + \frac{2}{1,000}$ in written form.

6 Write nine hundred one and seventy-five thousandths in expanded form.

Circle the letter for the correct answer.

7 Which of the following shows 17.201 in expanded form?

   A $17 + \frac{2}{10} + \frac{0}{100} + \frac{1}{1,000}$

   B seventeen and two hundred and one thousandth

   C $10 + 7 + \frac{2}{10} + \frac{1}{1,000}$

   D seventeen and two-tenths and one hundredth

8 Which of the following shows nine hundred and fifty-two thousandths in standard form?

   A 952,000

   B 900.52

   C 950.052

   D 900.052

Unit 3 Mini-Lesson ★
Compare and Order Decimals

Standard

Number, Operations, and Quantitative Reasoning

5.1B Use place value to read, write, compare, and order decimals through the thousandths place.

Model the Skill

Draw a place value chart on the board.

ones	.	tenths	hundredths	thousandths
0	.	4		
0	.	6		

◆ **Say:** *A place value chart can help you compare decimals. What are the decimals shown in this first place value chart?* (0.4 and 0.6) *Both numbers have the same number of digits and the same number of decimal places. How do you compare these numbers?* (Possible answer: Start at the digit on the left and compare the digits in the same place. If the digits are the same, move to the next digit to the right. Then compare the two digits to see which is greater.) *Which number is greater?* (0.6) *If 0.6 is greater than 0.4, then 0.4 is less than 0.6.*

◆ Assign students the appropriate practice page(s) to support their understanding of the skill.

Assess the Skill

Use the following problems to pre-/post-assess students' understanding of the skill.

0.71 ◯ 0.18   3.59 ◯ 5.39

4.81 ◯ 4.18   20.5 ◯ 50.2

6.07 ◯ 6.71   0.598 ◯ 0.589

STAAR Mathematics Practice Grade 5 • ©2013 Newmark Learning, LLC

Name _____   Date _____

Use a place value chart to compare numbers.
Write >, <, or = to complete each statement.

> is greater than
< is less than
= is equal to

ones	.	tenths	hundredths	thousandths
2	.	9		
3	.	2		

 ❶   2.9 ◯ 3.2   ❷   1.76 ◯ 1.67

❸   2.05 ◯ 2.11   ❹   31.08 ◯ 3.108

❺   1.01 ◯ 1.1   ❻   5.927 ◯ 5.927

❼   3.95 ◯ 4.35   ❽   0.86 ◯ 0.87

❾   2.9 ◯ 2.6   ❿   6.013 ◯ 6.08

 Tell how you know when two numbers are equal.

Name _____ **Date** _____

Use the symbols for greater than (>) or less than (<) to compare the numbers.

❶ 8.92 ◯ 8.9

❷ 8.92 ◯ 9.089

❸ 8.092 ◯ 8.9

❹ 8.92 ◯ 9.089

❺ 8.9 ◯ 9.089

❻ 8.092 ◯ 8.092

❼ 8.9 ◯ 9.089

❽ 8.09 ◯ 0.89

❾ 7.45 ◯ 7.54

❿ 2.3 ◯ 3.2

⓫ 1.9 ◯ 1.09

⓬ 0.68 ◯ 0.608

⓭ 4.05 ◯ 4.14

⓮ 5.2 ◯ .02

⓯ 7.063 ◯ 7.063

⓰ 9.2 ◯ 0.92

⓱ 0.285 ◯ 0.14

⓲ 0.25 ◯ 0.235

⓳ 1.9 ◯ 1.19

⓴ 3.15 ◯ 3.41

 Tell how you use a place value chart to compare numbers.

STAAR Mathematics Practice Grade 5 • ©2013 Newmark Learning, LLC

Name _____ Date _____

Solve.

1 Write a decimal that is less than 6.73.

2 Write a decimal that is greater than 0.04.

3 Write a decimal that is less than 5.89 and greater than 4.27.

4 Write a decimal that is greater than 3.3 and less than 3.73.

5 Tom paid $4.78 for his sandwich. Alicia paid $7.48 for a salad. Who paid more for lunch?

6 Marina bought 0.68 pound of American cheese and 0.82 pound of cheddar cheese. Which package of cheese weighed more?

Circle the letter for the correct answer.

7 Which statement is true?

    A 4.75 < 4.857 < 4.589

    B 4.75 < 4.589 < 4.857

    C 4.857 > 4.589 > 4.75

    D 4.589 < 4.75 < 4.857

8 Which statement is false?

    A 0.23 < 0.52 < 0.6

    B 1.7 < 2.1 < 4.3

    C 6.17 > 5.7 > 5.8

    D 0.9 > 0.89 > 0.869

Unit 4 Mini-Lesson
Add and Subtract Whole Numbers

Standard

Number, Operations, and Quantitative Reasoning

5.3A Use addition and subtraction to solve problems involving whole numbers and decimals.

5.14B Solve problems that incorporate understanding the problem, making a plan, carrying out the plan, and evaluating the solution for reasonableness.

Model the Skill

Write the following chart on the board.

Motor Vehicle Registrations (2005)

	Cars	Buses	Trucks
Texas	8,911,818	89,557	8,468,172

◆ **Ask:** *What is the total number of vehicles registered in Texas?* Guide students through the problem-solving process: understanding the problem, making a plan, carrying out the plan, and evaluating the solution for reasonableness

◆ **Say:** *Remember, we use place value to add and subtract.* Demonstrate how to align place values when using paper and pencil.

◆ **Ask:** *How many more cars than trucks were registered in 2005? Should we add or subtract to solve this problem?* Have students explain how to determine the operation. Then have students use the data in the chart to create and solve other word problems.

◆ Assign students the appropriate practice page(s) to support their understanding of the skill. You may allow students to use calculators.

Assess the Skill

Use the following problems to pre-/post-assess students' understanding of the skill.

5,126 + 4,730   10,487 + 6,418   1,000,000 + 1,500

2,650 – 947   50,525 – 5,000   100,000 – 40,800

STAAR Mathematics Practice Grade 5 • ©2013 Newmark Learning, LLC

Name _____ Date _____

Find the sum or difference for each problem.

1

millions			thousands			ones		
	1	0	2	5	0	7	0	0
+			8	6	9	3	5	8

2

millions			thousands			ones		
		1	0	0	0	0	0	0
−				2	5	9	5	0

---

3 6,789 + 14,352
```
    6,789
 + 14,352
 _____
```

4 3,650 + 9,275

---

5 865 + 786

6 208,900 + 800,650

7
```
     198
   5,215
+ 12,800
_____
```

8 23,650 – 9,275
```
  23,650
 – 9,275
 _____
```

---

9 5,723 – 5,285

10 8,436 – 684

---

11 17,609 – 7,365

12 100,000 – 93,205

 Tell how you used place value to add and subtract.

Name _____ **Date** _____

Find each sum or difference.

1 5,623 + 18,346

2 675,090 + 347,101

3 158,089 + 738,622

4 12,056 + 8,750

5 190,000 – 124,890

6 591,043 – 268,502

7
```
   567
+  823
```

8
```
 38,783
–   865
```

9
```
 9,511
–  703
```

10
```
 40,093
–   120
```

11
```
   762
+  593
```

12
```
 45,787
–   909
```

13
```
 6,041
–  250
```

14
```
 53,885
–   895
```

15
```
 1,270
–    95
```

16
```
 25,849
–   650
```

17
```
 7,090
–  143
```

18
```
 34,322
–   891
```

19
```
   659
+  278
```

20
```
 44,192
–   782
```

21
```
 3,253
–  412
```

22
```
 15,000
–   599
```

 Tell how you know your answer is reasonable.

Name _____ **Date** _____

Solve.

1 Team A collected 891 cans for recycling. Team B collected 1,259 cans. The teams want to reach a goal of 3,000 cans altogether. How many more cans do they need to collect?

2 Joe raised 1,355 dollars for a local charity. Jake raised 1,710 dollars for the same charity. How many more dollars did Jake raise for the charity?

3 The soccer stadium seats 24,000 spectators. 19,708 tickets were sold for the season playoff game. How many more seats are available?

4 Arlow has 2,035 dollars in her savings account. She deposits 195 more dollars. Then she withdraws 240 dollars of her savings to buy a new desk. How much money is left in her savings account?

Circle the letter for the correct answer.

5 Mount Rainier is 14,416 feet high. Mount Rainier is 5,667 feet higher than Guadalupe Peak. How high is Guadalupe Peak?

    A 20,083 ft

    B 9,749 ft

    C 8,749 ft

    D 5,667 ft

6 The distance from New York City to Houston is 1,419 miles by plane. Traveling by car it is 1,627 miles. How many more miles is the length of the trip by car?

    A 3,046 mi

    B 313 mi

    C 218 mi

    D 208 mi

Unit 5 Mini-Lesson ★
Add and Subtract Decimals

Number, Operations, and Quantitative Reasoning

5.3A Use addition and subtraction to solve problems involving whole numbers and decimals.

Model the Skill

Write the following problem on the board.

$$0.6 + 0.12 \qquad \begin{array}{r} 0.6 \\ + \quad 0.12 \\ \hline \end{array}$$

◆ Display a hundreds flat. **Say:** *Today we are going to see this as one whole. If this is one, what is a tens rod?* (one-tenth) *What is a ones cube?* (one-hundredth) *What is the sum of six-tenths and twelve-hundredths?* (seven-tenths and two-hundredths).

◆ Point to the vertical addition. **Ask:** *How do you add whole numbers?* (Add the columns starting on the right.) Guide students to add the decimals, starting with the hundredths place and regrouping as needed. **Say:** *The decimal points are lined up. Write a decimal point in the same position in the sum.* (0.72)

◆ Assign students the appropriate practice page(s) to support their understanding of the skill.

Assess the Skill

Use the following problems to pre-/post-assess students' understanding of the skill.

0.23 + 0.77	0.47 + 1.3	0.85 − 0.1
0.4 + 1.2	0.33 − 0.13	2.36 − 1.28
0.3 + 0.67	2.4 − 1.2	

Name _____ **Date** _____

Solve.

 1

	tens	ones	.	tenths	hundredths
		0	.	5	6
+		0	.	3	2

0.56 + 0.32

```
  0.56
+ 0.32
------
```

2

	tens	ones	.	tenths	hundredths
		0	.	9	0
−		0	.	1	1

0.9 – 0.11

```
  0.90
− 0.11
------
```

3

5.07 + 3.7

```
  5.07
+ 3.7
------
```

4

0.8 + 0.22

```
  0.80
+ 0.22
------
```

5

5.9 – 5.1

```
  5.9
− 5.1
-----
```

6

1.77 – 0.65

```
  1.77
− 0.65
------
```

7

0.78 + 0.27

```
  0.78
+ 0.27
------
```

8

0.41 + 0.87

```
  0.41
+ 0.87
------
```

9

0.28 – 0.14

```
  0.28
− 0.14
------
```

10

0.68 – 0.09

```
  0.68
− 0.09
------
```

11

1.98 + 1.9

```
  1.98
+ 1.90
------
```

12

3.52 – 0.61

```
  3.52
− 0.61
------
```

13

2.98 – 0.69

```
  2.98
− 0.69
------
```

14

9.38 – 0.93

```
  9.38
− 0.93
------
```

 Tell how you can use a place value chart to add decimals.

Name _____ **Date** _____

Solve.

1

1.7 + 0.38 = _____

2

2.6 – 0.72 = _____

3

3.65 + 1.52 = _____

4

40.7 – 0.38 = _____

5

15.06 + 10.5 = _____

6

5.06 – 1.9 = _____

7

7.8 – 4.08 = _____

8

20.6 + 20.01 = _____

9

4.33 – 0.43 = _____

10

17.3 – 3.4 = _____

11

6.02 + 0.89 = _____

12

6.33 + 0.63 = _____

13

9.8 – 2.12 = _____

14

9.08 + 3.62 = _____

15

4.03 – 3.37 = _____

16

1.56 + 1.64 = _____

17

5.36 + 1.44 = _____

18

10.1 + 1.01 = _____

19

7.6 – 0.93 = _____

20

2.85 – 0.81 = _____

21

4.93 + 4.62 = _____

22

12.8 + 0.02 = _____

23

3.8 – 3.42 = _____

24

508.1 – 37.61 = _____

 Tell how you can use addition to check your subtraction.

Name _____ **Date** _____

Solve.

1 What is the sum of 7.8 and 7.02?

2 What is the difference between 13.04 and 12.06?

---

3 Sara bought a loaf of bread for $3.49 and a gallon of milk for $4.50. How much more did the milk cost?

4 Jamal put $0.75 in the parking meter. An hour later, he added another $0.50. How much did he put in the meter in all?

---

5 The salmon weighs 8.5 pounds. The mackerel weighs 6.62 pounds. How much do the two fish weigh in all?

6 Keith jumps 7.25 feet on the standing long jump. Tanya jumps 6.62 feet. How much farther can Keith jump?

Circle the letter for the correct answer.

7 The race is 10 kilometers. Tom has run 7.43 kilometers so far. How much farther does he need to run in order to finish the race?

A 2.57 km

B 2.67 km

C 3.57 km

D 3.67 km

8 The first song in the dance routine is 1.75 minutes long. The second song is 2.5 minutes. What is the combined time of both songs?

A 2.0 minutes

B 3.8 minutes

C 3.25 minutes

D 4.25 minutes

Unit 6 Mini-Lesson
Identify Factors and Multiples

Standard

Number, Operations, and Quantitative Reasoning

5.3D Identify common factors of a set of whole numbers.

Model the Skill

Write the following multiplication sentences on the board.

$$1 \times 6 = 6$$
$$2 \times 3 = 6$$

◆ **Say:** *Factors are numbers that you multiply to get a product. Look at these number sentences.* Point to a factor (1, 6, 2, or 3). *What are factor pairs?* (the two numbers you multiply). *What factor pairs can I multiply to get a product of 6?* (1 and 6, or 2 and 3) Have students use six counters to model factor pairs showing one group of 6, six groups of 1, two groups of 3, and three groups of 2.

◆ **Ask:** *Can we make any more factor pairs for 6?* (no) *So what are the factors of 6?* (1, 2, 3, 6) Lead students to see that each factor of a number divides that number without a remainder.

◆ Assign students the appropriate practice page(s) to support their understanding of the skill. Point out that some numbers have only 2 factors, 1 and the number. You may wish to tell students that these numbers have a special name. They are called prime numbers.

Assess the Skill

Use the following problems to pre-/post-assess students' understanding of the skill.

◆ **Ask:** *How old are you?* List the factors of that number. Then list the first 5 multiples of that number.

Name _____ Date _____

Complete each chart. Then list the first 5 multiples for each number.

❶

0 x 3	1 x 3	2 x 3	3 x 3	4 x 3
0	3	6	_____	_____

factors of 3: _____, _____ multiples of 3: 0, 3, 6, _____, _____

❷

0 x 5	1 x 5	2 x 5	3 x 5	4 x 5
0	5	_____	_____	_____

factors of 5: _____, _____ multiples of 5: 0, 5, _____, _____, _____, _____

❸

0 x 7	1 x 7	2 x 7	3 x 7	4 x 7
_____	_____	_____	_____	_____

factors of 7: _____, _____, multiples of 7: _____, _____, _____, _____

❹

0 x 10	1 x 10	2 x 10	3 x 10	4 x 10
_____	_____	_____	_____	_____

factors of 10: _____, _____, _____, _____

multiples of 10: _____, _____, _____, _____, _____

 Tell how you can skip count to find multiples.

Name _____ **Date** _____

List the next 6 multiples for each number.

1 factors of 4: _____, _____, _____

multiples of 4: 0, 4, _____, _____, _____, _____, _____, _____

2 factors of 6: _____, _____, _____, _____

multiples of 6: 0, 6, _____, _____, _____, _____, _____, _____

3 factors of 2: _____, _____,

multiples of 2: 0, _____, _____, _____, _____, _____, _____

4 factors of 5: _____, _____

multiples of 5: 0, _____, _____, _____, _____, _____, _____

5 factors of 9: _____, _____, _____

multiples of 9: 0, _____, _____, _____, _____, _____, _____

 Tell how you can skip count to find multiples.

STAAR Mathematics Practice Grade 5 • ©2013 Newmark Learning, LLC

Name _____   **Date** _____

Solve.

1 Jane is making a list of the factors for the number 17. She will use 1 line in her notebook for each factor. How many lines will she use?

2 Phil is making a list of the factors for the number 24. He will use 1 line in his notebook for each factor. How many lines will he use?

3 List the multiples of 6 that are less than 30.

4 What is the lowest common multiple for the numbers 2 and 4?

Circle the letter for the correct answer.

5 Which of the following numbers is not a factor of 36?

    A 36

    B 8

    C 6

    D 4

6 Which of the following numbers is not a multiple of 8?

    A 16

    B 24

    C 40

    D 74

Unit 7 Mini-Lesson
Multiply Whole Numbers

Standard

Number, Operations, and Quantitative Reasoning

5.3B Use multiplication to solve problems involving whole numbers (no more than three digits times two digits) without technology.

Model the Skill

◆ Write the following multiplication problem on the board.

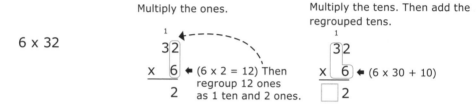

6 x 32

◆ **Say:** *There are different methods for multiplying numbers. Today we are going to focus on the short form.*

◆ **Ask:** *What do you need to do first to find the product of 32 and 6?* (Multiply the ones: 2 x 6 = 12) *How should we record 12 ones?* Guide students to regroup as 1 ten and 2 ones, recording the 2 ones as part of the answer and the 1 ten as a carry number. Have students multiply tens, reminding them to add the regrouped ten. Help students record the product (192) and understand that it represents (6 x 30) + (6 x 2).

◆ Assign students the appropriate practice page(s) to support their understanding of the skill.

Assess the Skill

Use the following problems to pre-/post-assess students' understanding of the skill.

7 x 97	21 x 345
49 x 57	43 x 803
62 x 81	221 x 40

Name _____ **Date** _____

Find the product for each problem.

Think:
(5 x 2) + (5 x 30)

Think:
(20 x 2) + (20 x 30)

1 32 x 25

```
  32
x 25
 160
```
← Multiply by the ones digit.

```
  32
x 25
 160
+640
```
← Multiply by the tens digit. (20 x 32)

← Add the partial products.

2 22 x 54
```
  54
x 22
```

3 12 x 31
```
  31
x 12
```

4 25 x 60
```
  60
x 25
```

5 49 x 57
```
  57
x 49
```

6 15 x 370
```
 370
x 15
```

7 82 x 160
```
 160
x 82
```

8 27 x 474
```
 474
x 27
```

9 38 x 615
```
 615
x 38
```

10 14 x 913
```
 913
x 14
```

11 64 x 327
```
 327
x 64
```

12 50 x 761
```
 761
x 50
```

13 43 x 807
```
 807
x 43
```

☆ **Tell why you might need to add to find a product.**

Name _____ **Date** _____

Find the product for each problem.

1
```
    53
x  56
```

2
```
    85
x  32
```

3
```
    50
x  28
```

4
```
    96
x  45
```

5
```
    73
x  16
```

6
```
    75
x  22
```

7
```
    49
x  19
```

8
```
    88
x  27
```

9
```
   233
x   26
```

10
```
   445
x   62
```

11
```
   203
x   11
```

12
```
   340
x   47
```

13
```
   313
x   42
```

14
```
   175
x   68
```

15
```
   593
x   31
```

16
```
   192
x   52
```

17
```
   771
x   21
```

18
```
   842
x   17
```

19
```
   253
x   31
```

20
```
   703
x   12
```

21
```
   336
x   30
```

22
```
   405
x   26
```

23
```
    93
x  79
```

24
```
   919
x   37
```

 Explain how you use place value when you multiply.

STAAR Mathematics Practice Grade 5 • ©2013 Newmark Learning, LLC

Name _____   **Date** _____

Solve.

1 Our class bought 24 tickets to the train show. Each ticket was $27.00. How much did the tickets cost in all?

2 There are 52 weeks in a year. If Kendra runs 12 miles every week, how many miles will she run in a year?

3 The property is 382 meters long and 89 meters wide. What is the area of the property?

4 The factory workers make 715 toys per day. If they work 5 days per week, how many toys will the workers make in 3 weeks?

5 The class has 31 textbooks. Each textbook has 576 pages. How many pages are there in all?

6 At top speed, the space shuttle can move as fast as 7,860 meters per second. At this rate, how many meters can it travel in a minute?

Circle the letter for the correct answer.

7 There are 124 guests at the charity fund-raiser. Each guest donates $85 to the charity. How much will money will the charity raise?

    A $10,540

    B $10,520

    C $10,510

    D $10,440

8 What is the product of 2,304 and 91?

    A 207,360

    B 209,664

    C 207,594

    D 186,624

Unit 8 Mini-Lesson
Divide by a One-Digit Divisor

Number, Operations, and Quantitative Reasoning

5.3C (RS) Use division to solve problems involving whole numbers (no more than two-digit divisors and three-digit dividends) without technology, including interpreting the remainder within a given context.

Model the Skill

Think:
4)9

```
   2
4)96   ← Divide tens. Then
  80      multiply.
       (20 x 4 = 80)
```

Think:
4)16

```
   2
4)96   ← Subtract. (96 - 80 = 16)
 -80
  16   ← Divide ones.
```

```
   24
4)96
 -80
  16   ← Multiply. (4 x 4 = 16)
 -16
   0   ← Subtract. (16 – 16 =
```

◆ **Ask:** *What is the quotient of 96 divided by 4?* (24)

◆ **Ask:** *How do you know?* (Possible answer: I divided the tens and the ones column in the dividend and found the quotient.) *How can you use multiplication to check division?* (Possible answer: Multiply the quotient by the divisor and see if you get the dividend.)

◆ Assign students the appropriate practice page(s) to support their understanding of the skill.

Assess the Skill

Use the following problems to pre-/post-assess students' understanding of the skill.

98 ÷ 7   2,345 ÷ 5
570 ÷ 6   803 ÷ 4
620 ÷ 8   5,067 ÷ 9

Name _____ Date _____

Divide. Show your work.

1 726 ÷ 3 = _____

$\begin{array}{r} 2 \\ 3\overline{)726} \\ -\ 600 \\ \hline 126 \end{array}$ ← Divide hundreds. ← Multiply. ← Then subtract.	$\begin{array}{r} 24 \\ 3\overline{)726} \\ -\ 600 \\ \hline 126 \\ -\ 120 \\ \hline 6 \end{array}$ Think: $3\overline{)12}$ ← Divide tens. ← Multiply. ← Then subtract.	$\begin{array}{r} 24 \\ 3\overline{)726} \\ -\ 600 \\ \hline 126 \\ -\ 120 \\ \hline 6 \\ -\ \underline{} \end{array}$ ← Divide ones. ← Multiply. ← Subtract.

2 78 ÷ 6 $6\overline{)78}$ **3** 63 ÷ 3 $3\overline{)63}$ **4** 54 ÷ 2 $2\overline{)54}$

5 378 ÷ 6 $6\overline{)378}$ **6** 489 ÷ 3 $3\overline{)489}$ **7** 543 ÷ 3 $3\overline{)543}$

8 1,782 ÷ 6 $6\overline{)1,782}$ **9** 8,091 ÷ 5 $5\overline{)8,091}$ **10** 5,476 ÷ 2 $2\overline{)5,476}$

☆ **Tell how you can use multiplication to check your answer.**

Name _____ **Date** _____

Divide. Show your work.

❶
$724 \div 6 =$ _____

❷
$335 \div 5 =$ _____

❸
$8{,}982 \div 2 =$ _____

❹
$162 \div 6 =$ _____

❺
$367 \div 3 =$ _____

❻
$623 \div 7 =$ _____

❼
$129 \div 6 =$ _____

❽
$4{,}623 \div 3 =$ _____

❾
$1{,}621 \div 4 =$ _____

❿
$427 \div 3 =$ _____

⓫
$126 \div 5 =$ _____

⓬
$771 \div 3 =$ _____

⓭
$815 \div 5 =$ _____

⓮
$616 \div 4 =$ _____

⓯
$914 \div 8 =$ _____

⓰
$413 \div 7 =$ _____

⓱
$913 \div 9 =$ _____

⓲
$754 \div 3 =$ _____

⓳
$733 \div 9 =$ _____

⓴
$828 \div 7 =$ _____

㉑
$5{,}633 \div 6 =$ _____

㉒
$4{,}415 \div 5 =$ _____

㉓
$8{,}741 \div 6 =$ _____

㉔
$3{,}798 \div 3 =$ _____

 Tell the steps you took to find the quotient.

STAAR Mathematics Practice Grade 5 • ©2013 Newmark Learning, LLC

Name _____ Date _____

Solve.

1 Our school has 6 grades and 786 students. What is the average number of students in each grade?

2 We have 72 eggs. Each container holds a half dozen. How many containers do we need for the eggs?

3 The area of the driveway is 384 square meters. The width of the driveway is 4 meters. What is the length?

4 The dairy truck delivered 2,560 pints of whipping cream this week. If there are 8 pints in a gallon, how many gallons of whipping cream did the truck deliver?

5 The bus travels the same exact route each week, making 9 round trips from Springfield to Burlington. If the bus travels 3,105 miles each week, how long is the bus route?

6 The movie theater collected $5,274 in ticket sales on Tuesday. If each ticket cost $9.00, how many tickets did the theater sell?

Circle the letter for the correct answer.

7 The jeweler needs 7 inches of gold chain to make a bracelet. If the jeweler has 750 inches of chain, how many bracelets can she make?

    A 108

    B 107

    C 106

    C 100

8 What is the quotient of 2,304 divided by 8?

    A 290

    B 388

    C 288

    D 278

Unit 9 Mini-Lesson

Divide by a Two-Digit Divisor

Number, Operations, and Quantitative Reasoning

5.3C (RS) Use division to solve problems involving whole numbers (no more than two-digit divisors and three-digit dividends) without technology, including interpreting the remainder within a given context.

Model the Skill

◆ Write the following division problem on the board with the corresponding model.

48 ÷ 12

◆ **Ask:** *What is the quotient of 48 divided by 12?* (4)

◆ **Ask:** *How did you find the answer? What basic facts did you think about to help solve this problem?* (4 ÷ 1 and 8 ÷ 2) *How did you check your answer?* (multiply 12 by 4)

◆ Assign students the appropriate practice page(s) to support their understanding of the skill.

Assess the Skill

Use the following problems to pre-/post-assess students' understanding of the skill.

980 ÷ 17   4,543 ÷ 15
670 ÷ 62   8,030 ÷ 40
3,672 ÷ 18   5,067 ÷ 29

Name _____ **Date** _____

Divide. Show your work.

1   435 ÷ 15 = _____

$$\begin{array}{r} 2 \\ 15\overline{)435} \\ -\ 30 \\ \hline \end{array}$$

2   528 ÷ 88 = _____

$$88\overline{)528}$$

3   726 ÷ 33 = _____

$$33\overline{)726}$$

4   120 ÷ 15 = _____

$$15\overline{)120}$$

5   968 ÷ 44 = _____

$$44\overline{)968}$$

6   325 ÷ 13 = _____

$$13\overline{)325}$$

7   9,605 ÷ 85 = _____

$$85\overline{)9,605}$$

8   952 ÷ 56 = _____

$$56\overline{)952}$$

9   720 ÷ 24 = _____

$$24\overline{)720}$$

10   3,424 ÷ 16 = _____

$$16\overline{)3,424}$$

11   3,692 ÷ 52 = _____

$$52\overline{)3,692}$$

12   705 ÷ 47 = _____

$$47\overline{)705}$$

13   2,660 ÷ 38 = _____

$$38\overline{)2,660}$$

14   807 ÷ 30 = _____

$$30\overline{)807}$$

15   6,902 ÷ 43 = _____

$$43\overline{)6,902}$$

16   713 ÷ 20 = _____

$$20\overline{)713}$$

☆ **Tell how you can use multiplication to check your answer.**

Name _____ **Date** _____

Divide. Show your work.

❶

8,775 ÷ 45 = _____

❷

3,006 ÷ 30 = _____

❸

1,037 ÷ 61 = _____

❹

9,058 ÷ 14 = _____

❺

2,072 ÷ 56 = _____

❻

4,005 ÷ 45 = _____

❼

1,872 ÷ 24 = _____

❽

1,675 ÷ 67 = _____

❾

9,020 ÷ 22 = _____

❿

4,472 ÷ 52 = _____

⓫

759 ÷ 23 = _____

⓬

8,075 ÷ 19 = _____

⓭

9,476 ÷ 46 = _____

⓮

8,833 ÷ 44 = _____

⓯

5,520 ÷ 23 = _____

⓰

8,575 ÷ 35 = _____

⓱

6,076 ÷ 56 = _____

⓲

894 ÷ 24 = _____

⓳

5,753 ÷ 11 = _____

⓴

3,990 ÷ 42 = _____

㉑

10,653 ÷ 53 = _____

㉒

9,943 ÷ 61 = _____

㉓

3,537 ÷ 27 = _____

㉔

6,080 ÷ 4 = _____

 Tell about what strategies you used to find the quotient.

STAAR Mathematics Practice Grade 5 • ©2013 Newmark Learning, LLC

Name _____ Date _____

Solve.

1 The theater has 352 seats. If there are 22 equal rows of seats, how many seats are in each row?

2 The perimeter of the bathroom is 372 inches. If there are 12 inches in a foot, what is the perimeter of the bathroom in feet?

3 If a space shuttle is traveling at 17,460 miles per hour, how fast is it moving per minute?

4 The area of the gym floor is 6,536 square feet. The length of the floor is 76 feet. What is the width?

5 The orchard sold 7,440 ounces of cherries last month. If there are 16 ounces in a pound, how many pounds of cherries did the orchard sell?

6 The lumberyard sold 4,480 cubic feet of wood last week. If it sold 35 cords of wood in all, how many cubic feet are in a cord?

Circle the letter for the correct answer.

7 Last summer, we drove cross-country. The road trip was a total of 6,765 miles. If we drove the same distance each day for 33 days, what was the average number of miles we drove each day?

A 25

B 250

C 205

D 215

8 Priscilla earned 781 dollars babysitting last year. If she charges 11 dollars per hour, how many hours did she babysit?

A 78

B 77

C 76

D 71

Unit 10 Mini-Lesson ★
Estimate Solutions

Standard

Number, Operations, and Quantitative Reasoning

5.4A (SS) Use strategies, including rounding and compatible numbers, to estimate solutions to addition, subtraction, multiplication, and division problems.

5.14A Identify the mathematics in everyday situations.

Model the Skill

◆ *When you do not need an exact answer, you can estimate by using rounding or compatible numbers.* Help students recall how to round a number to its greatest place. Point out that when estimating quotients, using compatible numbers is often easier than rounding.

◆ *What if you had 5 crates, each weighing 187 pounds. Could you take all of the crates on an elevator in one trip, if the elevator can carry 1,000 pounds?* Discuss how to estimate the solution. Remind students that they need to include their weight, also. *So, what would you do in this situation?*

◆ *We use estimation all the time in everyday life, especially when we are at the store and want to know if we have enough money to buy things.* Write the following problem on the board:

At the grocery store you pick up bread at $3.79, orange juice at $2.99, and eggs at $1.49. You also want some chips for $1.29. Can you buy all of that for $10? (yes, but it is close)

◆ *What are some other situations where you are likely to use estimation?* Help students create and solve estimation problems. Point out that we also use estimation to know whether our exact answers are reasonable.

◆ Assign students the appropriate practice page(s) to support their understanding of the skill.

Assess the Skill

Use the following problems to pre-/post-assess students' understandings of the skill.

Estimate.

7,890 + 4,376	10,487 + 17,418	2,750 – 1,947
43 x 17	518 x 4	237 ÷ 3

Name _____ **Date** _____

Use rounding to estimate each sum, difference, or product.

1

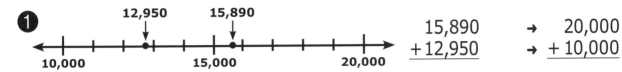

$$
\begin{array}{r}
15,890 \\
+\,12,950 \\
\end{array}
\quad
\begin{array}{r}
\rightarrow \quad 20,000 \\
\rightarrow \quad +\,10,000 \\
\hline
\end{array}
$$

Estimate

2 $\begin{array}{r} 7,746 \rightarrow \boxed{} \\ +\,2,198 \rightarrow \boxed{} \\ \hline + \end{array}$

3 $\begin{array}{r} 13,257 \rightarrow \boxed{} \\ \times\,5,048 \rightarrow \boxed{} \\ \hline \times \end{array}$

4 $\begin{array}{r} 24,129 \rightarrow \boxed{} \\ \times\,6,023 \rightarrow \boxed{} \\ \hline \times \end{array}$

5 $\begin{array}{r} 91,344 \rightarrow \boxed{} \\ -\,3,978 \rightarrow \boxed{} \\ \hline - \end{array}$

6 $\begin{array}{r} 60,894 \rightarrow \boxed{} \\ -\,18,755 \rightarrow \boxed{} \\ \hline - \end{array}$

7 $\begin{array}{r} 13,881 \rightarrow \boxed{} \\ -\,4,699 \rightarrow \boxed{} \\ \hline - \end{array}$

8 $\begin{array}{r} 22,067 \rightarrow \boxed{} \\ +\,16,900 \rightarrow \boxed{} \\ \hline + \end{array}$

9 $\begin{array}{r} 56,783 \rightarrow \boxed{} \\ \times\,4,289 \rightarrow \boxed{} \\ \hline \times \end{array}$

10 $\begin{array}{r} 608,988 \rightarrow \boxed{} \\ -\,31,732 \rightarrow \boxed{} \\ \hline - \end{array}$

11 $\begin{array}{r} 254,879 \rightarrow \boxed{} \\ +\,331,617 \rightarrow \boxed{} \\ \hline + \end{array}$

Use compatible numbers to estimate each quotient.

12 $4,582 \div 899$

_____ ÷ _____ = _____

13 $22,933 \div 3,784$

_____ ÷ _____ = _____

14 $61,795 \div 27,441$

_____ ÷ _____ = _____

15 $154,900 \div 459$

_____ ÷ _____ = _____

☆ **Tell how you used basic facts to find compatible numbers.**

Name _____ Date _____

Estimate the solution for each problem.

1 6.29 + 9.99
Estimate: _____

2 3.69 + 4.39
Estimate: _____

3 2.99 + 5.79
Estimate: _____

4 11.09 + 3.97
Estimate: _____

5 5.49 + 1.09
Estimate: _____

6 0.49 + 7.59
Estimate: _____

7 5.25 + 13.99
Estimate: _____

8 6.79 + 22.95
Estimate: _____

9 15.87 + 34.99
Estimate: _____

10 15.05 + 17.99
Estimate: _____

11 14.29 + 175.95
Estimate: _____

12 59.85 + 62.99
Estimate: _____

Use the price list to estimate the cost.

13 About how much does a gallon of milk and a dozen eggs cost altogether?

14 About how much more does a case of water cost than a gallon of milk?

15 If you buy 3 dozen eggs, about how much will you spend?

16 If you buy a bag of apples and 3 donuts, about how much change will you get back from $20.00?

Price List	
Apples (bag)	**$5.79**
Water (case)	**$12.39**
Milk (1 gallon)	**$4.18**
Eggs (1 dozen)	**$2.99**
Donuts (each)	**$0.89**

 For Problem 7, tell how you estimated the product.

Name _____ Date _____

Estimate to solve.

1 Barre has 4 items in her grocery basket that are $3.99, one item that is $7.99, and two things that are $2.29. About how much money will she need to pay for what's in her basket?

2 The band ordered 4 large pizzas for a practice dinner. Each pizza is $11.98 with tax. About how much money will the band need to pay for the pizzas?

3 Cole orders a turkey sandwich for $4.69, a roast beef on rye, which is $5.49, and 2 drinks at $1.79 each. If he gives the cashier a twenty-dollar bill, about how much money will he get back as change?

4 Serena has collected 3,890 stamps. Erika has collected three times that amount. About how many more stamps has Erika collected?

5 A gallon of milk costs $3.89, a loaf of bread costs $2.68, and a pound of butter costs $4.29. If Elana purchases 2 of each item, about how much money will she need?

6 There are 186 students who will need to ride buses to the regional playoffs. If 30 students fit on each bus, about how many buses will the event need?

Circle the letter for the correct answer.

7 Lucienne wants to buy party favors for her birthday. If each favor is $4.27 with tax, and she has 12 friends attending her party, about how much money will she spend on party favors?

- **A** $50
- **B** $60
- **C** $30
- **D** $70

8 A total of 1,578 people signed up for the blood drive. If each person gets 3 cookies, and 2 cups of juice, about how many cookies and cups should the Red Cross stock to prepare for the event?

- **A** 500 cookies and 750 cups
- **B** 1,500 cookies and 2,500 cups
- **C** 4,800 cookies and 3,200 cups
- **D** 4,500 cookies and 3,000 cups

Unit 11 Mini-Lesson

Relate Decimals to Fractions

Standard

Number, Operations, and Quantitative Reasoning

5.2D (SS) Use models to relate decimals to fractions that name tenths, hundredths, and thousandths.

Model the Skill

Draw the following models on the board or use manipulatives.

◆ **Say:** *These models represent decimals and fractions. Both decimals and fractions can name a part of one whole.*

◆ **Ask:** *How would you write a decimal to describe the shaded part of each model? (0.1, 0.01, 0.001) How would you write a fraction to describe the shaded part of each model? (1/10, 1/100, 1/1,000) Record the answers next to the models and label with the word names, one tenth, one hundredth, and one thousandth. Have students shade models and write a fraction and a decimal to describe the part they shaded.*

◆ **Ask:** *What decimal is equivalent to the fraction 1/2? (0.5) How can you show that on a tenths model?* Guide students to understand that decimal equivalents must have denominators of 10, 100, 1,000 and so on.

◆ Assign students the appropriate practice page(s) to support their understanding of the skill.

Assess the Skill

Use the following problems to pre-/post-assess students' understandings of the skill.

Write a fraction and decimal for each shaded part.

Name _____ **Date** _____

Write a fraction and a decimal for each shaded part.

① decimal: 0.3
fraction: _____

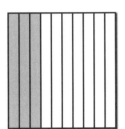

② decimal: _____
fraction: 1/100

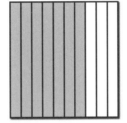

③ decimal: 0.005
fraction: _____

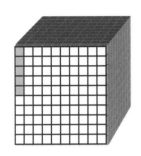

④ decimal: _____
fraction: _____

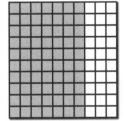

⑤ decimal: _____
fraction: _____

⑥ decimal: _____
fraction: _____

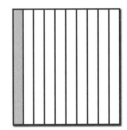

⑦ decimal: _____
fraction: _____

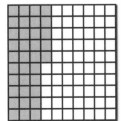

⑧ decimal: _____
fraction: _____

⑨ decimal: _____
fraction: _____

Name _____ **Date** _____

Write a fraction and a decimal for each shaded part.

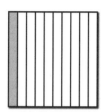

decimal: _____

fraction: _____

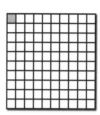

decimal: _____

fraction: _____

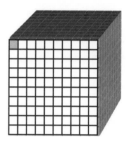

decimal: _____

fraction: _____

Write an equivalent fraction or decimal for each problem.

4
0.18 = _____

5
0.7 = _____

6
0.04 = _____

7
0.92 = _____

8
0.10 = _____

9
0.5 = _____

10
0.69 = _____

11
10.009 = _____

12
0.75 = _____

13
$\frac{3}{10}$ = _____

14
$\frac{1}{2}$ = _____

15
$\frac{4}{10}$ = _____

16
$\frac{5}{1000}$ = _____

17
$\frac{22}{100}$ = _____

18
$\frac{17}{1000}$ = _____

19
$\frac{60}{1000}$ = _____

 Give some examples of decimal and fraction equivalents using coins less than one dollar.

Name _____ **Date** _____

Solve.

1 Sara had one dollar. At the school store she spent $0.15 for a pencil and $0.60 for a banana. What fraction of a dollar does she have left?

2 The school has 100 students in the sixth grade. 53 of the students are girls. Write a fraction that shows the number of girls. Then write an equivalent decimal.

3 Ten students entered an essay contest. Two of the students who entered earned prizes for their writing. What fraction of the students earned writing prizes?

4 Of one thousand people surveyed in the last election, 550 were registered members of a political party. The rest were independent. Write a decimal that shows the portion of people surveyed who were independent.

5 Two hundred violinists were polled in a recent study. 130 of them were right-handed. Write a fraction that shows the portion of total violinists who were right-handed.

6 Of the left-handed violinists, only 3 use their left hands to bow. Write a decimal that shows what portion of the 200 violinists bow with their left hand.

7 Which decimal is equivalent to 7/10?

    A 7.10

    B 0.710

    C 0.7

    D 0.07

8 Which fraction best describes the model below?

    A $\dfrac{24}{100}$

    B 0.25

    C $\dfrac{25}{1000}$

    D $\dfrac{1}{4}$

Unit 12 Mini-Lesson ★
Find Equivalent Fractions

Standard	
	Number, Operations, and Quantitative Reasoning
	5.2A (RS) Generate a fraction equivalent to a given fraction such as 1/2 and 3/6 or 4/12 and 1/3.

Model the Skill

Hand out fraction bars and draw the following model on the board.

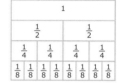

◆ **Say:** *Today we are going to learn about equivalent fractions. Equivalent fractions are fractions that are equal—they name the same amount.* Have students use fraction bars to model one-half. **Say:** *We want to see how many fourths it takes to equal one-half.* Have students use fraction bars to model the fourths.

◆ **Ask:** *How many fourths are equal to one-half? How do you know?* (2. It takes two-fourths to be the same size as one-half.) **Say:** *One-half and two-fourths are the same size. One-half and two-fourths are equivalent fractions.* You might suggest that students place the fourths on top of the half as another way to show they are equal.

◆ Assign students the appropriate practice page(s) to support their understanding of the skill.

Assess the Skill

Use the following problems to pre-/post-assess students' understanding of the skill.

$$\frac{1}{2} = \frac{\square}{4} \qquad \frac{1}{2} = \frac{\square}{6} \qquad \frac{1}{2} = \frac{\square}{8} \qquad \frac{1}{2} = \frac{\square}{10}$$

$$\frac{3}{6} = \frac{\square}{2} \qquad \frac{3}{4} = \frac{\square}{8} \qquad \frac{1}{4} = \frac{\square}{8} \qquad \frac{2}{4} = \frac{\square}{2}$$

STAAR Mathematics Practice Grade 5 • ©2013 Newmark Learning, LLC

Name _____ **Date** _____

Use fraction bars or a number line. Write equivalent fractions.

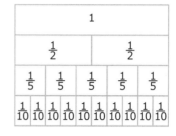

1							
$\frac{1}{2}$				$\frac{1}{2}$			
$\frac{1}{4}$		$\frac{1}{4}$		$\frac{1}{4}$		$\frac{1}{4}$	
$\frac{1}{8}$	$\frac{1}{8}$	$\frac{1}{8}$	$\frac{1}{8}$	$\frac{1}{8}$	$\frac{1}{8}$	$\frac{1}{8}$	$\frac{1}{8}$

1		
$\frac{1}{3}$	$\frac{1}{3}$	$\frac{1}{3}$
$\frac{1}{6}$ $\frac{1}{6}$	$\frac{1}{6}$ $\frac{1}{6}$	$\frac{1}{6}$ $\frac{1}{6}$

❶ $\dfrac{1}{3}$ = $\dfrac{\square}{\square}$

❷ $\dfrac{2}{3}$ = $\dfrac{\square}{\square}$

❸ $\dfrac{3}{3}$ = $\dfrac{\square}{\square}$

❹ $\dfrac{1}{2}$ = $\dfrac{\square}{\square}$

❺ $\dfrac{1}{4}$ = $\dfrac{\square}{\square}$

❻ $\dfrac{3}{4}$ = $\dfrac{\square}{\square}$

❼ $\dfrac{2}{8}$ = $\dfrac{\square}{\square}$

❽ $\dfrac{4}{8}$ = $\dfrac{\square}{\square}$

❾ $\dfrac{6}{8}$ = $\dfrac{\square}{\square}$

❿ $\dfrac{2}{10}$ = $\dfrac{\square}{\square}$

⓫ $\dfrac{4}{10}$ = $\dfrac{\square}{\square}$

⓬ $\dfrac{6}{10}$ = $\dfrac{\square}{\square}$

 Tell how you know the fractions are equivalent.

Name _____ **Date** _____

Use fraction bars or a number line. Write equivalent fractions.

1 $\dfrac{2}{3} = \dfrac{\square}{\square}$

2 $\dfrac{1}{4} = \dfrac{\square}{\square}$

3 $\dfrac{2}{5} = \dfrac{\square}{\square}$

4 $\dfrac{3}{6} = \dfrac{\square}{\square}$

5 $\dfrac{4}{4} = \dfrac{\square}{\square}$

6 $\dfrac{6}{8} = \dfrac{\square}{\square}$

7 $\dfrac{2}{6} = \dfrac{\square}{\square}$

8 $\dfrac{4}{8} = \dfrac{\square}{\square}$

9 $\dfrac{6}{6} = \dfrac{\square}{\square}$

10 $\dfrac{6}{10} = \dfrac{\square}{\square}$

11 $\dfrac{4}{6} = \dfrac{\square}{\square}$

12 $\dfrac{5}{10} = \dfrac{\square}{\square}$

13 $\dfrac{2}{8} = \dfrac{\square}{\square}$

14 $\dfrac{1}{3} = \dfrac{\square}{\square}$

15 $\dfrac{4}{5} = \dfrac{\square}{\square}$

 Explain how you find equivalent fractions.

Name _____ **Date** _____

Solve.

 A pizza has 8 slices. One-half of the pizza has meatballs. How many slices have meatballs?

$$\frac{1}{2} = \frac{?}{8}$$

 The fruit bowl has 6 apples. Half of the apples are green. How many apples are green?

$$\frac{1}{2} = \frac{?}{6}$$

③ Robin has some bananas. 6 bananas are ripe. Three-fifths of the bananas are ripe. How many bananas does Robin have in all?

$$\frac{3}{5} = \frac{6}{?}$$

④ Tate has 4 dollars in her wallet. One-half of her dollars are in her wallet. How many dollars does she have in all?

$$\frac{1}{2} = \frac{4}{?}$$

⑤ Which of the following fractions is equal to one-half?

A $\frac{4}{6}$

B $\frac{2}{3}$

C $\frac{4}{2}$

D $\frac{2}{4}$

⑥ Nils has 9 pages in the chapter. He has read 3 pages. How much of the chapter has he read?

A $\frac{9}{3}$

B $\frac{1}{2}$

C $\frac{1}{4}$

D $\frac{1}{3}$

Unit 13 Mini-Lesson
Generate Mixed Numbers and Improper Fractions

Standard

Number, Operations, and Quantitative Reasoning

5.2B (SS) Generate a mixed number equivalent to a given improper fraction or generate an improper fraction equivalent to a mixed number.

Model the Skill

Draw the following circles on the board.

- ◆ **Say:** *We write a mixed number as a whole number and a fraction.* **Ask:** *What mixed number describes the shaded part of the circles?* $(1\frac{1}{2})$

- ◆ **Say:** *An improper fraction has a numerator greater than or equal to the denominator.* **Ask:** *What improper fraction describes the shaded part of the circles?* $(\frac{3}{2})$

- ◆ **Say:** *One and one half and three halves are equivalent. Write $1\frac{1}{2} = \frac{3}{2}$ on the board under the circles.* Remind students how to write one whole as a fraction, i.e. $\frac{2}{2}, \frac{5}{5}, \frac{27}{27}$. Then demonstrate how to convert an improper fraction to a mixed number by dividing the numerator by the denominator.

- ◆ **Ask:** *How can we convert a mixed number like $3\frac{1}{4}$ to an improper fraction?* Guide student to see how multiplying the whole number by the denominator and adding the numerator yields the equivalent improper fraction. Draw a picture to show $3\frac{1}{4} = \frac{13}{4}$.

- ◆ Assign students the appropriate practice page(s) to support their understanding of the skill.

Assess the Skill

Use the following problems to pre-/post-assess students' understanding of the skill.

Write an equivalent improper fraction or mixed number for each.

$$2\frac{1}{3} \quad 1\frac{5}{8} \quad 4\frac{3}{4} \quad \frac{8}{3} \quad \frac{11}{6} \quad \frac{13}{10}$$

 STAAR Mathematics Practice Grade 5 • ©2013 Newmark Learning, LLC

Name _____ **Date** _____

Write each mixed number as an improper fraction.

 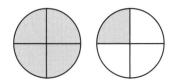

mixed number: $1\frac{1}{4}$

improper fraction: _____

 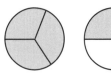

mixed number: $1\frac{2}{3}$

improper fraction: _____

  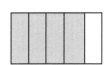

mixed number: $1\frac{4}{5}$

improper fraction: _____

 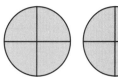

mixed number: $2\frac{3}{4}$

improper fraction: _____

5 mixed number: $1\frac{1}{2}$

improper fraction: _____

6 mixed number: $3\frac{1}{3}$

improper fraction: _____

Write each improper fraction as a mixed number.

improper fraction: $\frac{11}{6}$

mixed number: _____

improper fraction: $\frac{12}{5}$

mixed number: _____

9 improper fraction: $\frac{5}{2}$

mixed number: _____

10 improper fraction: $\frac{4}{3}$

mixed number: _____

11 improper fraction: $\frac{9}{4}$

mixed number: _____

12 improper fraction: $\frac{13}{3}$

mixed number: _____

 Tell how you know when a fraction is an improper fraction.

Name _____ **Date** _____

Write an equivalent improper fraction or mixed number for each.

 1

improper fraction: $\frac{9}{4}$

mixed number: _____

 2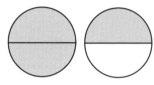

improper fraction: $\frac{3}{2}$

mixed number: _____

 3

mixed number: $1\frac{1}{3}$

improper fraction: _____

 4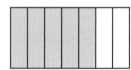

mixed number: $1\frac{5}{7}$

improper fraction: _____

5 mixed number: $4\frac{1}{4}$

improper fraction:_____

6 mixed number: $3\frac{1}{3}$

improper fraction:_____

7 improper fraction: $\frac{11}{6}$

mixed number: _____

8 improper fraction: $\frac{12}{5}$

mixed number: _____

9 improper fraction: $\frac{5}{2}$

mixed number: _____

10 improper fraction: $\frac{4}{3}$

mixed number: _____

11 improper fraction: $\frac{9}{4}$

mixed number: _____

12 improper fraction: $\frac{13}{3}$

mixed number: _____

13 improper fraction: $\frac{12}{8}$

mixed number: _____

14 improper fraction: $\frac{15}{14}$

mixed number: _____

15 mixed number: $4\frac{7}{8}$

improper fraction:_____

16 mixed number: $5\frac{2}{9}$

improper fraction:_____

☆ **Tell how you know when a fraction is an improper fraction.**

STAAR Mathematics Practice Grade 5 • ©2013 Newmark Learning, LLC

Name _____ **Date** _____

Solve.

1 What improper fraction is equivalent to $4\frac{2}{3}$?

2 Convert $\frac{46}{12}$ to a mixed number.

3 What mixed number is equivalent to $\frac{33}{15}$?

4 Convert $\frac{60}{7}$ to a mixed number.

5 What mixed number is equivalent to $\frac{23}{3}$?

6 What improper fraction is equivalent to $9\frac{4}{5}$?

Circle the letter for the correct answer.

7 Luis bought $3\frac{5}{6}$ pounds of grapes. What improper fraction is equivalent to the amount of grapes he bought?

A $3\frac{10}{12}$

B $\frac{35}{6}$

C $\frac{23}{6}$

D $\frac{32}{6}$

8 Alexis is converting the mixed number $7\frac{4}{11}$ to an improper fraction. What number should she put as the numerator?

A 81

B 28

C 77

D 39

Unit 14 Mini-Lesson ★
Compare Fractions to Solve Problems

Standard

Number, Operations, and Quantitative Reasoning

5.2C (RS) Compare two fractional quantities in problem-solving situations using a variety of methods, including common denominators.

Model the Skill

Write the following pairs of fractions on the board.

$\frac{3}{8}$ and $\frac{5}{8}$ $\frac{1}{2}$ and $\frac{5}{6}$ $\frac{2}{3}$ and $\frac{1}{4}$ $\frac{2}{6}$ and $4\frac{1}{2}$

◆ **Ask:** *What can you tell me about the denominators of the first set of fractions?* (the same or common) *How can we compare the fractions?* (compare the numerators; $\frac{3}{8} < \frac{5}{8}$)

◆ **Ask:** *How can we compare the second set of fractions? What should we do first?* (find a common denominator: 6) *What do we do next?* (write an equivalent fraction for $\frac{1}{2}$ with 6 as the denominator; $\frac{1}{2} = \frac{3}{6}$, then compare the numerators.) If students are struggling, you may wish to have them use fraction strips to find equivalents.

◆ **Say:** *Now look at the third set of fractions. We need to find a common denominator and write equivalent fractions for both numbers in order to compare them.* Help students write and compare fractions using the symbols <, >, and =.

◆ For the fourth set of fractions, guide students to simplify fractions first, if possible, before comparing or finding a common denominator.

◆ Assign students the appropriate practice page(s) to support their understanding of the skill.

Assess the Skill

Use the following problems to pre-/post-assess students' understanding of the skill.

Compare. Use <, >, or =.

$\frac{4}{8} \bigcirc \frac{6}{12}$ $\frac{5}{7} \bigcirc \frac{2}{7}$ $\frac{2}{3} \bigcirc \frac{5}{9}$ $\frac{1}{4} \bigcirc \frac{1}{3}$

$\frac{4}{10} \bigcirc \frac{2}{5}$ $\frac{5}{16} \bigcirc \frac{3}{8}$ $\frac{3}{4} \bigcirc \frac{10}{12}$ $\frac{1}{5} \bigcirc \frac{2}{6}$

Name _____ Date _____

Use a common denominator to write equivalent fractions for each set of fractions.

1 $\frac{3}{4}$ and $\frac{1}{2}$

_____ and _____

2 $\frac{5}{8}$ and $\frac{1}{4}$

_____ and _____

3 $\frac{2}{5}$ and $\frac{1}{10}$

_____ and _____

4 $\frac{2}{3}$ and $\frac{1}{2}$

_____ and _____

5 $\frac{1}{4}$ and $\frac{3}{5}$

_____ and _____

6 $\frac{3}{9}$ and $\frac{4}{12}$

_____ and _____

Use >, <, or = to compare fractions. Find a common denominator if necessary.

7 $\frac{2}{3}$ ◯ $\frac{4}{8}$

8 $\frac{2}{5}$ ◯ $\frac{6}{15}$

9 $\frac{14}{16}$ ◯ $\frac{3}{5}$

10 $\frac{7}{10}$ ◯ $\frac{12}{18}$

11 $\frac{3}{4}$ ◯ $\frac{5}{6}$

12 $\frac{6}{8}$ ◯ $\frac{2}{3}$

13 $\frac{8}{15}$ ◯ $\frac{4}{7}$

14 $\frac{2}{12}$ ◯ $\frac{3}{15}$

15 $\frac{4}{8}$ ◯ $\frac{10}{16}$

16 $\frac{2}{5}$ ◯ $\frac{9}{12}$

17 $\frac{6}{7}$ ◯ $\frac{9}{10}$

18 $\frac{1}{3}$ ◯ $\frac{3}{8}$

19 $\frac{12}{18}$ ◯ $\frac{2}{3}$

20 $\frac{6}{12}$ ◯ $\frac{4}{10}$

21 $\frac{3}{12}$ ◯ $\frac{3}{15}$

☆   **Tell how to find a common denominator for Problem 4.**

Name _____ **Date** _____

Use >, <, or = to compare fractions. Find a common denominator if necessary.

1 $\dfrac{3}{10}$ ◯ $\dfrac{1}{3}$ **2** $\dfrac{7}{8}$ ◯ $\dfrac{1}{2}$ **3** $\dfrac{4}{5}$ ◯ $\dfrac{3}{4}$

4 $\dfrac{4}{12}$ ◯ $\dfrac{3}{10}$ **5** $\dfrac{5}{6}$ ◯ $\dfrac{7}{8}$ **6** $\dfrac{3}{5}$ ◯ $\dfrac{12}{18}$

7 $\dfrac{7}{14}$ ◯ $\dfrac{2}{5}$ **8** $\dfrac{8}{9}$ ◯ $\dfrac{7}{8}$ **9** $\dfrac{5}{9}$ ◯ $\dfrac{3}{5}$

10 $\dfrac{3}{4}$ ◯ $\dfrac{12}{16}$ **11** $\dfrac{1}{5}$ ◯ $\dfrac{2}{20}$ **12** $\dfrac{6}{8}$ ◯ $\dfrac{2}{5}$

13 $\dfrac{1}{5}$ ◯ $\dfrac{2}{12}$ **14** $\dfrac{2}{6}$ ◯ $\dfrac{3}{18}$ **15** $\dfrac{4}{8}$ ◯ $\dfrac{2}{3}$

16 $\dfrac{5}{18}$ ◯ $\dfrac{4}{10}$ **17** $\dfrac{10}{20}$ ◯ $\dfrac{16}{20}$ **18** $\dfrac{2}{7}$ ◯ $\dfrac{3}{10}$

19 $\dfrac{11}{12}$ ◯ $\dfrac{9}{10}$ **20** $\dfrac{4}{8}$ ◯ $\dfrac{6}{12}$ **21** $\dfrac{3}{4}$ ◯ $\dfrac{8}{15}$

22 $\dfrac{5}{10}$ ◯ $\dfrac{15}{20}$ **23** $\dfrac{6}{11}$ ◯ $\dfrac{4}{7}$ **24** $\dfrac{2}{3}$ ◯ $\dfrac{5}{8}$

☆ **Tell the steps you took to compare the fractions in Problem 7.**

STAAR Mathematics Practice Grade 5 • ©2013 Newmark Learning, LLC

Name _____ **Date** _____

Solve.

① Luke and Gia have the same number of math problems for homework. Gia has $\frac{7}{8}$ of her math homework completed. Luke has $\frac{3}{4}$ of his math homework done. Who has completed more of the homework?

② Tess read 6 pages of her chapter. The chapter was 10 pages long. Amelia completed 5 pages of a 12-page chapter. Who read a greater portion of her chapter?

③ Hannah and Charlie are running a 5K. Hannah is $\frac{2}{3}$ of the way finished. Charlie has run 3 of the 5 kilometers. Who has run farther?

④ It takes 1 hour to drive to Vita and Dom's grandmother's house. They are $\frac{3}{4}$ of the way there. How many minutes do they still have to travel?

⑤ On Monday, Dari had ten dollars in her wallet. She spent seven dollars and fifty cents on lunch. What fraction of the money in her wallet did she spend on lunch?

⑥ On Wednesday, Dari had seven dollars in her wallet. She spent six dollars on lunch. On which day did she spend a greater fraction of the money in her wallet on lunch—Monday or Wednesday?

Circle the letter for the correct answer.

⑦ Jason is going for a 7-mile run. He has completed 5/10 of the run. How many miles has he run so far?

    A 5

    B $5\frac{1}{2}$

    C $3\frac{1}{2}$

    D $\frac{1}{2}$

⑧ There were two dozen eggs in the fridge. Jake used six eggs to make omelettes. He then scrambled half of the remaining eggs. What fraction of the total eggs are left?

    A $\frac{1}{2}$

    B $\frac{1}{3}$

    C $\frac{3}{4}$

    D $\frac{3}{8}$

Unit 15 Mini-Lesson ★
Add and Subtract Fractions

Standard

Number, Operations, and Quantitative Reasoning

5.3E (SS) Model situations using addition and/or subtraction involving fractions with like denominators using concrete objects, pictures, words, and numbers or fractions referring to the same whole and having like denominators, e.g., by using visual fraction models and equations to represent the problem.

Model the Skill

- ◆ Draw $\frac{1}{3}$ + $\frac{1}{3}$ + $\frac{1}{3}$ on the board.

- ◆ **Say:** *Today we are going to add like fractions. Like fractions have the same denominator.* **Ask:** *What do we do when we add like fractions?* (add the numerators) *What is the sum of* $\frac{1}{3}$ + $\frac{1}{3}$ + $\frac{1}{3}$ *?* ($\frac{3}{3}$ or 1)

- ◆ **Ask:** *What is the sum of* $\frac{2}{3}$ + $\frac{1}{3}$ *?* ($\frac{3}{3}$) *How do you know?* Draw models and discuss how $\frac{3}{3}$ can be visualized as $\frac{2}{3}$ + $\frac{1}{3}$. **Say:** *We can decompose any fraction into a sum of its parts.*

- ◆ Draw $\frac{2}{4}$ + $\frac{1}{4}$ + $\frac{1}{4}$ on the board. *Look at this problem. What is the sum?* ($\frac{4}{4}$ or 1) *How do you know?*

- ◆ Assign students the appropriate practice page(s) to support their understanding of the skill.

Assess the Skill

Use the following problems to pre-/post-assess students' understanding of the skill.

$\frac{2}{8}$ + $\frac{5}{8}$ $\qquad$ $\frac{1}{6}$ + $\frac{2}{6}$ $\qquad$ $\frac{2}{5}$ + $\frac{2}{5}$

$\frac{1}{4}$ − $\frac{1}{4}$ $\qquad$ $\frac{7}{10}$ − $\frac{4}{10}$ $\qquad$ $\frac{5}{12}$ − $\frac{4}{12}$

Name _____ **Date** _____

Solve.

 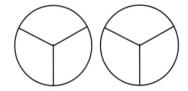

$\dfrac{2}{3}$ + $\dfrac{2}{3}$ = _____ or _____

$\dfrac{3}{4}$ − $\dfrac{1}{4}$ = _____ or _____

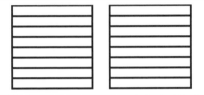

$\dfrac{5}{8}$ + $\dfrac{5}{8}$ = _____ or _____

$\dfrac{5}{6}$ − $\dfrac{3}{6}$ = _____ or _____

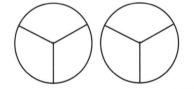

$\dfrac{2}{3}$ + $\dfrac{3}{3}$ = _____ or _____

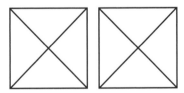

$\dfrac{3}{4}$ + $\dfrac{2}{4}$ = _____ or _____

$\dfrac{5}{8}$ − $\dfrac{5}{8}$ = _____ or _____

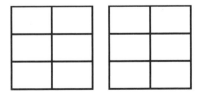

$\dfrac{4}{6}$ + $\dfrac{6}{6}$ = _____ or _____

 Tell how you subtract fractions.

Name _____ **Date** _____

Solve.

1

$$\frac{3}{3} - \frac{1}{3} = \underline{\hspace{1cm}}$$

2

$$\frac{2}{3} + \frac{2}{3} = \underline{\hspace{1cm}}$$

3

$$\frac{1}{4} + \frac{1}{4} = \underline{\hspace{1cm}}$$

4

$$\frac{3}{4} - \frac{1}{4} = \underline{\hspace{1cm}}$$

5

$$\frac{5}{7} - \frac{2}{7} = \underline{\hspace{1cm}}$$

6

$$\frac{4}{7} + \frac{2}{7} = \underline{\hspace{1cm}}$$

7

$$\frac{1}{5} - \frac{1}{5} = \underline{\hspace{1cm}}$$

8

$$\frac{3}{5} + \frac{1}{5} = \underline{\hspace{1cm}}$$

9

$$\frac{3}{10} + \frac{1}{10} = \underline{\hspace{1cm}}$$

10

$$\frac{9}{10} - \frac{6}{10} = \underline{\hspace{1cm}}$$

11

$$\frac{4}{5} + \underline{\hspace{1cm}} = \frac{7}{5}$$

12

$$\frac{4}{5} - \underline{\hspace{1cm}} = \frac{2}{5}$$

 Write the sums for Problems 2 and 11 as mixed numbers.

Name _____ **Date** _____

Solve each problem. Show your work. Draw a picture to help.

❶ Linda planted $\frac{2}{10}$ of the garden with red roses. She planted $\frac{3}{10}$ of the garden with pink roses and $\frac{1}{10}$ of the garden with yellow roses. What part of the garden was planted with roses?

❷ So far, the team has won $\frac{5}{10}$ of their games. They lost $\frac{3}{10}$ of their games and tied $\frac{1}{10}$ of their games. What portion of their game schedule have they played so far?

❸ $\frac{5}{8}$ of the tables in the cafe are round. $\frac{3}{8}$ are square. How many more of the tables are round tables?

❹ $\frac{8}{10}$ of the seats in the theater are dark blue. $\frac{2}{10}$ of the seats are light blue. How many more seats are dark blue?

Circle the letter for the correct answer.

❺ Kristen made some pies for the bake sale. 4/8 of the pies are strawberry rhubarb. 2/8 of the pies are pecan. How much greater a portion of the pies are strawberry rhubarb?

    A one-quarter

    B one-half

    C one-eighth

    D six-eighths

❻ Which of the following mixed numbers is equal to $\frac{8}{6}$?

    A $1\frac{1}{3}$

    B $2\frac{1}{2}$

    C $2\frac{2}{6}$

    D $2\frac{1}{3}$

Unit 16 Mini-Lesson ★

Describe Relationships

Standard

Patterns, Relationships, and Algebraic Reasoning

5.5A (RS) Describe the relationship between sets of data in graphic organizers such as lists, tables, charts, and diagrams.

5.15A Explain and record observations using objects, words, pictures, numbers, and technology.

Model the Skill

Write the following table on the board.

Input	Output
3	6
5	10
7	14
9	18

◆ **Say:** *We are going to look for patterns in tables and lists today. We want to see if there is a relationship between the numbers, and if so, determine how to describe it.*

◆ **Ask:** *In this table, how would you describe the relationship of the output number to the input number? Is the output increasing or decreasing?* (increasing) *By how much?* (2 times more than the input) *Does that relationship hold true for each pair of input and output numbers?* (yes)

◆ **Say:** *We can describe what we observe by writing a rule. The rule for this table is that output is 2 times more than input. Each output number equals the input multiplied by 2.* Write the rule next to the table, and then write 17 in the input column.

◆ **Ask:** *How can we use the rule for this table to find the output for 17?* (multiply: 17 x 2 = 34) Erase the output numbers and give a new rule for output, such as add 2 to the input. Help students complete the table according to the new rule. Continue in this fashion until students are comfortable observing and explaining relationships.

◆ Assign students the appropriate practice page(s) to support their understanding of the skill.

Assess the Skill

Use the following problems to pre-/post-assess students' understanding of the skill.

Describe the relationship.

Input	Output
25	22
20	17
15	12
10	7

Input	Output
3	15
4	16
5	17
6	18

STAAR Mathematics Practice Grade 5 • ©2013 Newmark Learning, LLC

Name _____ **Date** _____

Complete each table. Then write a rule to describe the relationship between input and output.

 ❶

Input	Output
2	8
3	12
4	16
5	20

rule:_____

 ❷

Input	Output
3	1
12	4
24	8
36	

rule:_____

 ❸

Input	Output
40	25
60	45
80	65
90	

rule:_____

 ❹

Input	Output
41	35
38	32
35	29
32	

rule:_____

 ❺

Book Sale Price List	
Number of Books	Price
2	3.50
3	5.25
4	7.00
5	

rule:_____

 ❻

Gallons of Gas	Number of Miles
2	62
3	93
4	124
6	

rule:_____

 ☆ **Tell how you found the rule for Problem 4.**

Name _____ Date _____

Write a rule to describe the relationship between input and output.

 ①

Input	Output
45	32
50	37
60	47
85	72

rule: _____
_____

 ②

Input	Output
6	14
7	16
8	18
9	20

rule: _____
_____

③

Input	Output
60	30
76	38
92	46
108	

rule: _____
_____

 ④

Pet, Inc. Price List	
Cans of Dog Food	Price
3	2.00
6	4.00
9	6.00
12	

rule: _____
_____

 ⑤

Pizza Topping Price List	
# of Toppings	Price
1	9.25
2	11.00
3	13.75
5	

rule: _____
_____

⑥

Paint Price List	
Gallons of Paint	Price
1	18.00
2	35.00
3	52.00
4	69.00
5	

rule: _____
_____

⑦

Input	Output
5	7
10	17
15	27
20	37
40	

rule: _____
_____

⑧

Input	Output
78	40
52	27
26	14
10	

rule: _____
_____

⑨

Input	Output
12	39
15	48
20	63
25	

rule: _____
_____

 ⑩

Flour Needed for Pancake Breakfast						
Cups of Flour	2					
Number of Servings	6					

rule: _____
_____

 Tell how you found the amount of flour needed to make pancakes for 75 people.

Name _____ Date _____

Solve.

 1 A store gives $10 cash back for every $50 spent. Ava makes the following list.

Spend	Get Back
$50	$10
$100	$20
$150	$30

Based on her list, what will Ava's final cost be for $200 spent on clothes?

 2 The paint store is having a sale. The store will give you half off every second gallon of paint.

# of Gal.	Price
1	$22
2	$33
3	$55

Based on this price list, how much will 8 gallons of paint cost?

 3 Jared's credit card charges a $5 fee for every $100.00 borrowed. Jared makes a chart.

$ on Credit Card	Fee
$100	$5.00
$200	$10.00
$300	$15.00

Based on his chart, what will Jared's charge be if he borrows $840 on his credit card this month?

4 The bigger the ketchup bottle, the better the savings. This chart shows how the price per ounce decreases as the number of ounces increases.

Oz. of Ketchup	Price
8 oz.	$3.20
16 oz.	$5.60
24 oz.	

Based on this rate, what will 24 ounces of ketchup cost?

Circle the letter for the correct answer.

 5 Marc is training for a marathon. He wants to increase the number of miles he runs by the same amount each week. The table below shows the total number of miles he runs each week.

Week	Number of Miles
1	8
2	9
3	10
4	
5	12

Based on the information in the table, how many miles did he run in the 4th week?

A The number of miles run is 3 times more than the number of weeks.

B The number of miles run is 1 more than the number of weeks.

C The number of miles run is 7 times more than the first week.

D The number of miles run is 7 more than the number of weeks.

Unit 17 Mini-Lesson
Identify Prime and Composite Numbers

Standard

Patterns, Relationships, and Algebraic Reasoning

5.5B (SS) Identify prime and composite numbers using concrete objects, pictorial models, and patterns in factor pairs.

5.14D Use tools such as real objects, manipulatives, and technology to solve problems.

Model the Skill

Draw the following rectangles on the board.

◆ **Say:** *All whole numbers except 0 and 1 are either prime numbers or composite numbers.* Discuss that a **prime number** is greater than 1 and has only two factors, itself and 1. A **composite number** has more than two factors.

◆ **Ask:** *What whole number does the first rectangle represent?* (2) *What pair of factors can you write that is equal to 2?* (1 x 2) *Is 2 prime or composite?* (prime). Give students tiles or graph paper and have them build or draw different rectangles for 3, 4, 5, and 6.

◆ **Ask:** *Which rectangles on the board represent composite numbers?* (4, 6) *How do you know?* Guide students to see that they can build two different rectangles for 4 (1 x 4; 2 x 2) and 6 (1 x 6; 2 x 3). Write the factor pairs for each picture under the picture.

◆ Assign students the appropriate practice page(s) to support their understanding of the skill.

Assess the Skill

Use the following problems to pre-/post-assess students' understanding of the skill.

Write whole number factor pairs for each number. Then identify each number as prime or composite.

7   8   10   13   28   31   35   37   42   43

    STAAR Mathematics Practice Grade 5 • ©2013 Newmark Learning, LLC

Name _____ **Date** _____

Write factor pairs for each number. Tell if the number is prime or composite. Use tiles or drawings to help.

❶

Factor Pairs for 9
1 x 9
3 x _____

Factors of 9:

9 is a _____ number.

❷

Factor Pairs for 12
1 x 12
2 x _____
_____ x _____

Factors of 12:

12 is a _____ number.

❸

Factor Pairs for 14
_____ x _____
_____ x _____

Factors of 14:

14 is a _____ number.

❹

Factor Pairs for 17
_____ x _____
_____ x _____

Factors of 17:

17 is a _____ number.

❺

Factor Pairs for 21
_____ x _____
_____ x _____

Factors of 21:

21 is a _____ number.

❻

Factor Pairs for 7
_____ x _____
_____ x _____

Factors of 7:

7 is a _____ number.

❼

Factor Pairs for 15
_____ x _____
_____ x _____

Factors of 15:

15 is a _____ number.

❽

Factor Pairs for 23
_____ x _____
_____ x _____

Factors of 23:

23 is a _____ number.

☆ **Tell how you know if a number is a prime number.**

Name _____ **Date** _____

Identify each number as prime or composite. Show your work.

1 8 is a _____ number.

2 11 is a _____ number.

3 61 is a _____ number.

4 21 is a _____ number.

5 19 is a _____ number.

6 9 is a _____ number.

7 51 is a _____ number.

8 45 is a _____ number.

9 43 is a _____ number.

10 3 is a _____ number.

11 87 is a _____ number.

12 1 is a _____ number.

13 63 is a _____ number.

14 16 is a _____ number.

15 92 is a _____ number.

 Tell how you can determine if 37 is prime or composite.

Name _____ **Date** _____

Solve.

1 How many prime numbers are there between 1 and 20? List them.

2 How many prime numbers are there between 20 and 40? List them.

3 Is the number 83 prime or composite?

4 List all of the prime numbers between 40 and 50.

5 Is the number 87 prime or composite?

6 List all of the composite numbers between 70 and 80.

Circle the letter for the correct answer.

7 Which group lists all the whole number factors for the composite number 24?

    A 2, 4, 6, 8, 24

    B 2, 4, 6, 8, 12, 24

    C 1, 2, 3, 4, 6, 8, 12, 24

    D 1, 2, 4, 6, 8, 9, 12, 24

8 Which model below represents a prime number?

    A

    B

    C

    D

Unit 18 Mini-Lesson ★
Write Equations

Standard

Patterns, Relationships, and Algebraic Reasoning

5.6A Select from and use diagrams and equations such as $y = 5 + 3$ to represent meaningful problem situations.

Model the Skill

Write the following sentence on the board:

18 is equal to 3 times as many as 6.

◆ **Ask:** *How else can we write this sentence?* (18 is equal to 6 multiplied by 3, etc.) *How can we write this sentence using only numbers and symbols?*

◆ **Say:** *Think about the statement "3 times as many as." How does that help you know what operation to use?*

◆ Assign the appropriate practice page to support students' understanding of the skill. Focus on the language structure of the statements to help them yield corresponding equations. Remind students that a letter can stand for an unknown number in an equation. Remind them that an equation shows equal values on either side of the equal symbol.

Assess the Skill

Use the following problems to pre-/post-assess students' understanding of the skill.

◆ Write the following sentences on the board and ask students to write an equation for each one.

18 is equal to 3 times as many as 6.
7 groups of 6 items is the same as 42 items.
32 is 4 times as much as 8.
Some number is equal to 19 plus 6.

◆ Then ask students to write their own story problems. **Say:** *Complete the story. Then write an equation to represent the story.*

_____ pirates found a sunken treasure chest filled with gold coins. They split the coins evenly among them and each received _____ coins. How many coins were in the chest?

_____ x _____ = c

STAAR Mathematics Practice Grade 5 • ©2013 Newmark Learning, LLC

Name _____ Date _____

Write an equation to describe each statement. Use drawings to solve.

1 18 items separated into 3 equal groups is equal to some number of items in each group.

_____ ÷ _____ = _____

2 4 groups of 5 items is the same as 20 items.

_____ x _____ = _____

3 18 is 3 times more than 6.

_____

4 Some number divided by 5 is 4.

_____

5 5 groups of 5 items plus 1 item is the same as 26 items.

_____

6 393 is three times as much as some number.

_____

7 654 divided by some number is 218.

_____

8 Some number minus 6 is equal to 20 minus 19.

_____

 Tell how you know which operation symbol to use.

Name _____ **Date** _____

Write an equation to represent each problem. Then solve.

1 There are 8 books in each box.
There are 3 boxes. How many books
are there in all?

_____

2 There are 2 times as many shaded triangles
as white triangles. There are 3 white triangles.
How many triangles are shaded?

_____

3 Mike made 4 rows of counters.
He put 6 counters in each row.
How many counters did he use?

_____

4 A doll costs $17. A doll dress costs 8 dollars
less. How much does the doll dress cost?

_____

5 Chris returned cans to the recycling center
and got 5 cents for each can. Chris got
$4.50 in all. How many cans did Chris return?

_____

6 A T-shirt costs $6. A sweatshirt costs
5 times as much. How much does
the sweatshirt cost?

_____

7 Lori has 562 beads. She needs 30 beads
to make a necklace. How many necklaces
can she make?

_____

8 Kate has a $10 bill. She bought a pencil
case that cost $3.62. How much change
did she get back?

_____

 Tell how you know where to place the symbol for the unknown.

  STAAR Mathematics Practice Grade 5 • ©2013 Newmark Learning, LLC

Name _____ Date _____

Solve.

1 There are 3 school buses. Each bus has 8 students. How many students are on the buses?

_____ x _____ = _____

2 Soo used 32 seeds. She put 8 seeds in each row. How many rows did she make?

_____ ÷ _____ = _____

3 Leah has 48 cards. She puts 8 cards in each row. How many rows did she make?

_____

4 There are 18 books in the bookcase. There are 6 books on each shelf. How many shelves are there?

_____

Circle the letter for the correct answer.

5 Tommy has 36 tomato plants. He has 4 equal rows of plants. Which equation shows the number of plants in each row?

  A $36 + 4 = p$

  B $36 ÷ 4 = p$

  C $36 \times 4 = p$

  D $36 - 4 \times p = t$

6 Celia can type a whole page in 3 minutes. If she types for 22 minutes, which equation shows the number of whole pages she can type?

  A $22 \times 3 = p$

  B $22 - 3 = p$

  C $22 ÷ 3 = p$

  D $22 - 3 - 3 - 3 - 3 - 3 - 3 - 3 = p$

7 There are 6 more blue umbrellas than yellow umbrellas. Which equation shows the number of blue umbrellas?

  A $6 + y = b$

  B $6 \times b = y$

  C $6 \times y = b$

  D $y ÷ 6 = b$

8 Ms. Brown buys 3 new T-shirts for $27. The T-shirts each cost the same amount. Which equation shows the cost of one T-shirt?

  A $c = 27 - 3$

  B $c = 27 + 3$

  C $27 ÷ 3 = c$

  D $27 \times 3 = c$

Unit 19 Mini-Lesson ★
Classify Quadrilaterals

Standard	**Geometry and Spatial Reasoning** **5.7A (SS)** Identify essential attributes including parallel, perpendicular, and congruent parts of two- and three-dimensional geometric figures.

Model the Skill

◆ **Say:** *We are going to use properties of polygons.* Remind students that a polygon is a closed, flat shape with sides that are line segments. Have students list the names of as many polygons as they can.

◆ **Ask:** *What are some properties of polygons?* (number of sides and angles, congruent sides, parallel sides, right angles)

◆ Assign students the appropriate practice page(s) to support their understanding of the skill.

Assess the Skill

Use the following problems to pre-/post-assess students' understanding of the skill.

◆ Ask students to describe the following lines and angles.

◆ Ask students to label, sort, and classify the following figures and shapes.

◆ Ask students to define and draw examples of the following:

parallel lines
perpendicular lines
right angle
rectangle
quadrilateral

trapezoid
rhombus
similar rectangles
congruent quadrilaterals
line of symmetry

Name _____   **Date** _____

Use the dot paper to draw the figures.

1 Draw two different polygons that have four sides and four angles.

2 Draw two different quadrilaterals that have two pairs of congruent and parallel sides.

3 Draw a quadrilateral with exactly one pair of parallel sides.

4 Draw two similar triangles.

☆ **Tell how a rectangle is different from the quadrilateral you drew.**

Name _____ **Date** _____

Draw each figure.

1 a parallelogram with four right angles

2 a parallelogram with no right angles

3 a parallelogram with four congruent sides and four right angles

4 a parallelogram with two congruent sides and two congruent angles

5 a parallelogram with four congruent sides and two pairs of congruent angles

6 a quadrilateral with two parallel sides and two pairs of congruent angles

 Describe the properties of a parallelogram.

Name _____ Date _____

Classify each polygon into categories. Write as many categories that apply.

1 What are three names for a polygon that has four equal sides and no right angles?

_____

_____

2 What is the name of a polygon that has four sides and four equal angles?

_____

_____

---

3 Draw a polygon with only two congruent sides and two congruent angles.

4 Draw a polygon with only one set of parallel sides and no right angles.

Circle the letter for the correct answer.

5 Which of the following is not a defining property of parallelograms?

A four sides and four angles

B at least 1 set of parallel sides

C at least 1 set of equal angles

D at least 1 set of right angles

6 How would you describe the two figures below?

A similar

B congruent

C parallel

D perpendicular

Unit 20 Mini-Lesson ★
Classify Geometric Figures

Standard

Geometry and Spatial Reasoning

5.7A (SS) Identify essential attributes including parallel, perpendicular, and congruent parts of two- and three-dimensional geometric figures.

5.16A Make generalizations from patterns or sets of examples and nonexamples.

Model the Skill

◆ **Say:** *We can make a chart of attributes to help us classify two-dimensional figures.* Write the chart on the board and help students complete and extend the chart to include various triangles and pentagons. Group figures by the number of sides.

Figure	Number of Sides	Number of Angles	Congruent Sides	Parallel Sides	Number of Right Angles
Rectangle	4	4	Opposite sides	Opposite sides	4
Parallelogram	4	4	Opposite sides	Opposite sides	0

◆ **Ask:** *So how is a parallelogram different from a rectangle?* (no right angles) *Are any sides perpendicular?* (in a parallelogram, no, because no right angles)

◆ **Say:** *Now let's make a chart for three-dimensional figures.* Help students complete and extend the chart to include rectangular prism, triangular prism, pyramid, cone, and cylinder. You may wish to have geometric solids available for students to examine.

Figure	Number of Sides	Number of Vertices	Congruent Faces	Number of Edges	Parallel Edges	Perpendicular Edges
Cube	6 (square)	8	6	12	yes	yes

◆ Assign students the appropriate practice page(s) to support their understanding of the skill.

Assess the Skill

Use the following problems to pre-/post-assess students' understanding of the skill.

◆ Ask students to use attributes to describe the following figures.

right triangle	rectangular prism
trapezoid	cone
pentagon	cube

STAAR Mathematics Practice Grade 5 • ©2013 Newmark Learning, LLC

Name _____ Date _____

Complete the chart. Name the figure.

Symbols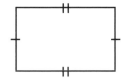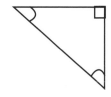

	Figure	Number of Sides	Number of Congruent Sides	Number of Angles	Number of Right Angles
❶					
❷					
❸					
❹					

❺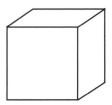

Number of faces _____
Shapes of faces _____
Pairs of opposite parallel faces _____
Number of vertices _____

❻

Number of faces _____
Shapes of faces _____
Pairs of opposite parallel faces _____
Number of vertices _____

☆ **A cube has perpendicular edges. Tell what that means.**

Name _____ **Date** _____

Circle the figure that does not belong in each set. Use attributes to explain your reasoning.

1
A   B   C   D

Reason _____

2
A   B   C   D

Reason _____

3
A   B   C   D

Reason _____

4
A   B   C   D

Reason _____

5
A   B   C   D

Reason _____

6
A   B   C   D

Reason _____

 Tell how a rectangle and a parallelogram are the same and how they are different.

Name _____ **Date** _____

How are these figures the same? How are they different?

 ❶

 ❷

❸

❹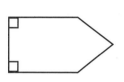

❺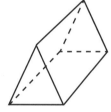

❻

Circle the letter for the correct answer.

❼ Which of the following statements does NOT describe a parallelogram?

A It has 2 pairs of congruent sides.

B It has 2 pairs of opposite parallel sides.

C It has 2 pairs of perpendicular sides.

D It has no right angles.

❽ Which of the following statements is true?

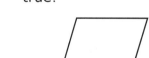

A Both figures have two acute angles.

B Both figures have at least one obtuse angle.

C Both figures have right angles.

D Both figures have obtuse angles.

Unit 21 Mini-Lesson ★

Locate Points on the Coordinate Plane

Standard

Geometry and Spatial Reasoning

5.9A Locate and name points on a coordinate grid using ordered pairs of whole numbers.

Model the Skill

◆ Draw the coordinate plane on the board and plot the following points.

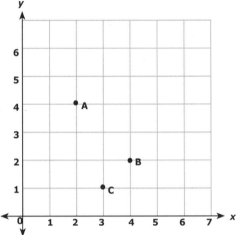

◆ *What do you know about a coordinate plane? What are coordinates? How are they used?* Record students' responses. Tell students that the plane is two-dimensional space and coordinates are the numbers that let us locate points in that space, like coordinates on a map or GPS.

◆ Have students look at the board and point to the grid, the lines or axes that form the grid, the horizontal *x*-axis, the vertical *y*-axis, and the origin where the axes meet.

◆ *We use ordered pairs to locate points. Ordered pairs are coordinates. The first number,* x, *tells how far to move along the x-axis. The second number in the ordered pair,* y, *tells how far to move along the* y-axis. Point A is at (2, 4). Have students locate the points at (4, 2) and (3, 1). Emphasize that order is important.

◆ Assign students the appropriate practice page(s) to support their understanding of the skill.

Assess the Skill

Use the following problems to pre-/post-assess students' understanding of the skill.

◆ Have students write ordered pairs for additional points on the coordinate plane.

Name _____ **Date** _____

Write the ordered pair for each point.

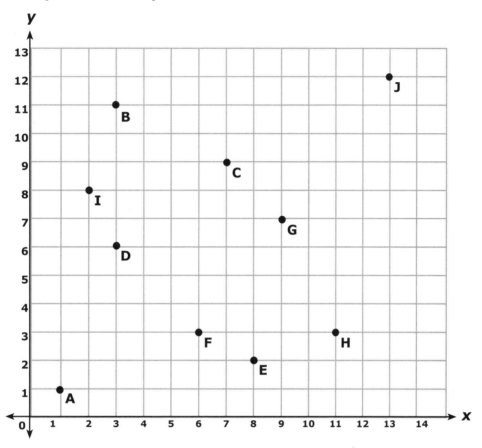

① Point A: (1, _____)

② Point B: (3, _____)

③ Point C: (_____, _____)

④ Point D: (_____, _____)

⑤ Point E: (_____, _____)

⑥ Point F: (_____, _____)

⑦ Point G: (_____, _____)

⑧ Point H: (_____, _____)

⑨ Point I: (_____, _____)

⑩ Point J: (_____, _____)

☆ **Tell how you write an ordered pair.**

Name _____ Date _____

Write the ordered pair for each point.

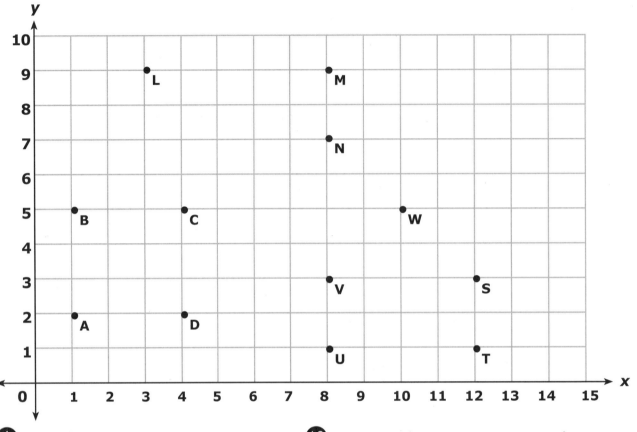

1️⃣ Point A: (_____, _____)

2️⃣ Point B: (_____, _____)

3️⃣ Point C: (_____, _____)

4️⃣ Point D: (_____, _____)

5️⃣ Point L: (_____, _____)

6️⃣ Point M: (_____, _____)

7️⃣ Point N: (_____, _____)

8️⃣ Point S: (_____, _____)

9️⃣ Point T: (_____, _____)

🔟 Point U: (_____, _____)

1️⃣1️⃣ Point V: (_____, _____)

1️⃣2️⃣ Point W: (_____, _____)

1️⃣3️⃣ **Connect points ABCD and describe the shape:** _____

1️⃣4️⃣ **Connect points LMN and describe the shape:** _____

1️⃣5️⃣ **Connect points STUVW and describe the shape:** _____

⭐ **Explain why the number of points can help you predict the type of polygon.**

Name _____   Date _____

Use the graph to solve the problems.

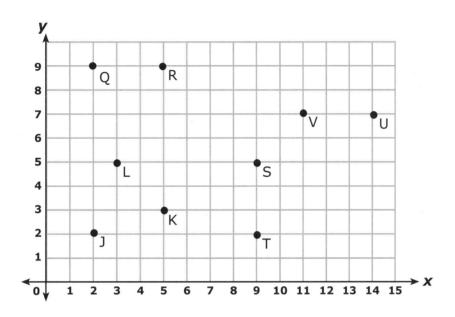

1 Write the ordered pair for point K.

2 Write the ordered pair for point L.

3 What ordered pair describes the location of point R?

4 What point has coordinates (14, 7)?

5 Connect points JKL and describe the shape.

6 What points can you connect to form a trapezoid?

Circle the letter for the correct answer.

7 Which point is located at (5, 9)?

    A Point K

    B Point L

    C Point S

    D Point R

8 What ordered pair describes the location of point V?

    A (14, 7)

    B (11, 7)

    C (12, 7)

    D (7, 11)

Unit 22 Mini-Lesson ★
Identify Transformations

Standard

Geometry and Spatial Reasoning

5.8A (RS) Sketch the results of translations, rotations, and reflections on a Quadrant I coordinate grid.

5.8B (SS) Identify the transformation that generates one figure from the other when given two congruent figures on a Quadrant I coordinate grid.

Model the Skill

◆ *Today we are going to use a coordinate grid to sketch congruent figures and identify transformations. We will start with one figure and move it by sliding, flipping, or rotating.* Draw the grid and triangle below.

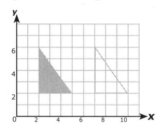

◆ *If we slide (translate) the triangle 5 units across the x-axis, what will the new triangle look like?* (same) *How can you describe its position?* (It has moved 5 units to the right, but not up or down.)

◆ *If we rotate (turn) the triangle, what will it look like?* Demonstrate a rotation on the grid.

◆ *If we flip (reflect) the triangle, what will it look like?* Students should recognize that the triangle and its reflected image are congruent.

◆ Point out that reflection, rotation, and translation are words that describe rigid motions, and together they are called transformations.

◆ Assign students the appropriate practice page(s) to support their understanding of the skill.

Assess the Skill

Use the following problems to pre-/post-assess students' understanding of the skill.

Have students identify the transformations.

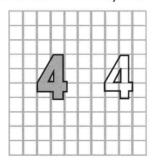

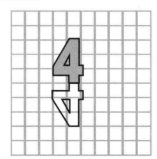

Name _____ **Date** _____

Sketch each transformation on the grid.

1

Translation

2

Reflection

3

Rotation

4

Translation and reflection

Write the type of transformation shown in each diagram.

5

_____

_____

6

_____

_____

Name _____ **Date** _____

Sketch each transformation on the grid.

 ❶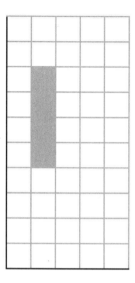

❷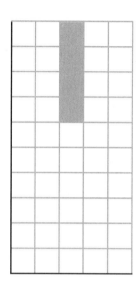

❸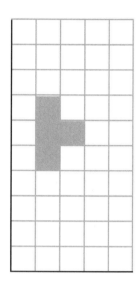

Translation

Rotation

Reflection

Identify each transformation.

 ❹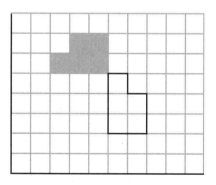

❺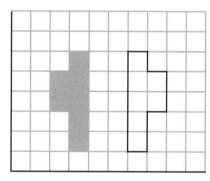

_____

_____

❻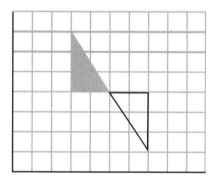

❼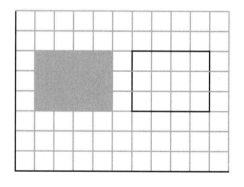

_____

_____ and _____

 ⭐ **Tell what you look for to identify a translation.**

STAAR Mathematics Practice Grade 5 • ©2013 Newmark Learning, LLC

Name _____ **Date** _____

Solve.

1 A single transformation was repeated several times to make the design below. Identify the transformation.

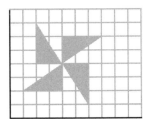

2 Use transformations to make a design on the grid below. Write the transformations you used.

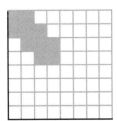

3 Sketch a rotation of the figure below.

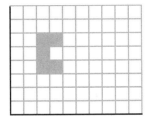

4 Sketch a reflection of the figure below.

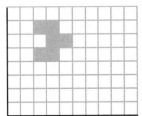

Circle the letter for the correct answer.

5 Which picture shows a single transformation labeled correctly?

A
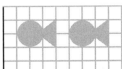
Reflection

B
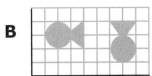
Rotation

C
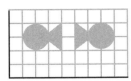
Reflection

D

Translation

Unit 23 Mini-Lesson ★
Convert Among Metric Units

Standard

Measurement

5.10A (SS) Perform simple conversions within the same measurement system (SI [metric] or customary).

Model the Skill

◆ **Ask:** *What are some units of length in the metric system?* Write the units and their abbreviations on the board (km, m, cm, mm). You may wish to include decameter (dm). Allow students to examine a cm ruler. Discuss that a millimeter is 1/10 of a centimeter and relate it to decimal notation. Be sure students understand the relative size of all the units of length.

◆ **Say:** *When we operate with units of length, we need to work with the same units, so sometimes we need to convert a smaller unit to a larger unit, or a larger unit to a smaller unit.*

◆ **Ask:** *How can we convert meters into centimeters?* (multiply by 100) *How can we convert centimeters into meters?* (divide by 100) Help students understand that when we multiply to convert from a larger unit to a smaller unit, we will get more smaller units. Conversely, when we divide, we will get fewer (or a part of) large units.

◆ Assign students the appropriate practice page(s) to support their understanding of the skill.

Assess the Skill

Use the following problems to pre-/post-assess students' understanding of the skill.

◆ Ask students to convert measurements to complete the following table.

Metric Units of Length			
10 millimeters		0.01 meter	0.00001 kilometer
100 millimeters	10 centimeters		0.0001 kilometer
1,000 millimeters		1 meter	
			1 kilometer

STAAR Mathematics Practice Grade 5 • ©2013 Newmark Learning, LLC

Name _____ **Date** _____

Complete each problem. Use the chart to help you.

	Metric Units of Mass

① 20 kilograms (kg) = _____ metric tons (t)

_____ ÷ _____ = _____

② 1,300 grams (g) = _____ kilograms (kg)

1 t = 1,000 kg
1 kg = 0.001 t

③ 9 kg = _____ g

_____ x _____ = _____

④ 50 kg = _____ t

1 kg = 1,000 g
1 g = 0.001 kg

⑤ 4,020 kg = _____ t

⑥ 7 g = _____ kg

⑦ 30 kg = _____ g

⑧ 10,500 kg = _____ t

☆ **Tell how you know your answers are correct.**

Name _____ **Date** _____

Complete each problem. Use the chart to help you.

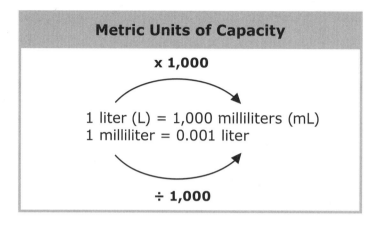

Metric Units of Capacity

x 1,000

1 liter (L) = 1,000 milliliters (mL)
1 milliliter = 0.001 liter

÷ 1,000

❶ 5 mL = _____ L

❷ 360 mL = _____ L

❸ 2,850 mL = _____ L

❹ 1,900 mL = _____ L

❺ 70 mL = _____ L

❻ 305 mL = _____ L

❼ 6 L = _____ mL

❽ 807 L = _____ mL

❾ 25.5 L = _____ mL

❿ 1,100 mL = _____ L

⓫ 450 mL = _____ L

⓬ 10 mL = _____ L

 Tell what to do when you want to convert from a smaller unit to a larger unit.

STAAR Mathematics Practice Grade 5 • ©2013 Newmark Learning, LLC

Name _____ Date _____

Solve each problem. Show your work.

1 The fish aquarium holds 150 liters of water. How many milliliters does the aquarium hold?

2 The mass of the boulder is 48,567 kilograms. What is the mass of the boulder in metric tons?

3 The pier is 200 meters long. Each board is 80 centimeters wide. How many boards are in the pier?

4 We rode our bikes 3,500 meters every day for 5 days. How many kilometers did we bike in all?

5 Felice caught 5.4 kilograms of fish this morning. Her dad caught 3,900 grams. How many kilograms of fish did they catch in all?

6 It is a 3-kilometer hike to the river. PJ walks for 500 meters. Then he walks another 1,050 meters. How many more kilometers must PJ hike to reach the river?

Circle the letter for the correct answer.

7 How many milliliters are in 35.05 liters?

    A 0.3505

    B 30,505

    C 35,500

    D 35,050

8 How many millimeters are in 20 meters?

    A 0.02

    B 2,000

    C 20,000

    D 200,000

Unit 24 Mini-Lesson ★
Convert Among Customary Units

Standard

Measurement

5.10A Perform simple conversions within the same measurement system (SI [metric] or customary).

Model the Skill

Customary Units of Length	
12 inches (in.) = 1 foot (ft)	36 inches = 1 yard
3 feet = 1 yard (yd)	5,280 feet = 1 mile (mi)

◆ **Ask:** *What are some units of length in the customary system?* Write the units and their abbreviations on the board (in., ft, yd, mi). Be sure students understand the relative size of all the units of length.

◆ **Say:** *When we operate with units of length in the customary system, we often mix units, like 5 feet 6 inches, or we use fractions, like $5\frac{1}{2}$ feet.* Have students look at the chart and discuss equivalents. Note that they are not powers of ten like in the metric system.

◆ **Ask:** *When we need to convert a smaller unit to a larger unit, what do you think we do?* (divide) *How many feet is 60 inches?* (5 ft) *What did you use as the divisor?* (12) *When we need to convert a larger unit to a smaller unit, what do you think we do?* (multiply) *How many feet is 4 yards?* (12 ft) *What did you use as the multiplier?* (3)

◆ Assign students the appropriate practice page(s) to support their understanding of the skill.

Assess the Skill

Use the following problems to pre-/post-assess students' understanding of the skill.

◆ Ask students to convert the following measurements to complete the table.

Customary Units of Length		
12 inches	**1 foot**	$\frac{1}{3}$ **yard**
36 inches		**1 yard**
5,280 feet		**1 mile**

STAAR Mathematics Practice Grade 5 • ©2013 Newmark Learning, LLC

Name _____ Date _____

Complete each problem.

Customary Units of Weight
16 ounces (oz) = 1 pound (lb)
2,000 pounds   = 1 ton (t)

1 6,000 lbs = _____ t

_____ ÷ _____ = _____

2 10,000 lbs = _____ t

---

3 64 oz = _____ lbs

4 100 oz = _____ lbs

_____ lbs and _____ oz

---

5 15 t = _____ lbs

_____ x _____ = _____

6 2 t = ____ oz

_____ x _____ x _____ = _____

---

7 $1\frac{1}{2}$ t = _____ lbs

8 $3\frac{1}{4}$ t = _____ lbs

---

9 28 oz = _____ lbs

10 5,000 lbs = _____ t

---

11 32 t = _____ lbs

12 65 oz = _____ lbs

 Tell how you know your answer is correct.

Name _____ **Date** _____

Complete each problem.

Customary Units of Capacity
8 fluid ounces (fl oz) = 1 cup (c)   2 pints = 1 quart (qt)
2 cups = 1 pint (pt)   4 quarts = 1 gallon (gal)

1 48 fl oz = _____ c

2 4 fl oz = _____ c

3 98 fl oz = _____ c

4 32 c = _____ pt

5 16 c = _____ qt

6 20 qt = _____ gal

7 2 gal = _____ qt

8 50 pt = _____ c

9 54 qt = _____ pt

10 1 gal = _____ oz

11 424 pt = _____ gal

12 10 gal = _____ qt

 Tell what to do when you want to convert from a smaller unit to a larger unit.

Name _____ Date _____

Solve each problem. Draw a picture to help you. Show your work.

① The window is 60 inches wide. What is the width of the window in feet?

② The perimeter of Jared's property is 56 yards. How many feet of fence will Jared need if he wants to enclose the whole property?

③ Each serving of oatmeal is 8 ounces. How many servings are in a 5-lb bag of oats?

④ The bottle of water contains 32 fluid ounces of water. How many cups of water are in the bottle?

⑤ We have 8 yards of wrapping paper. If we use 2 feet for each present, how many presents can we wrap?

⑥ Stephanie rides her bike 2 miles to the post office, and then another 50 yards to the train station. How many yards long was her trip?

Circle the letter for the correct answer.

⑦ How many gallons are in 500 pints?

    A 125

    B 62.5

    C 1,000

    D 4,000

⑧ If there are 5,280 feet in one mile, how many yards are in 2 miles?

    A 1,760

    B 10,560

    C 35,200

    D 3,520

Unit 25 Mini-Lesson ★
Find Perimeter and Area

Standard

Measurement

5.10B (SS) Connect models for perimeter, area, and volume with their respective formulas.

5.10C (RS) Select and use appropriate units and formulas to measure length, perimeter, area, and volume.

5.14B Solve problems that incorporate understanding the problem, making a plan, carrying out the plan, and evaluating the solution for reasonableness.

Model the Skill

◆ **Ask:** *How can we find the perimeter of our classroom?* (Measure the distance around the room where the wall meets the floor) *What unit of measure should we use?* (foot or meter) Allow students to measure each side and record the measurements, rounding to the nearest whole unit. Connect student measurements to the formula for perimeter of a rectangle: *P = 2l + 2w.*

◆ **Ask:** *How can we find the area of our classroom?* (Count the floor or ceiling tiles; multiply length x width). Remind students that area is the number of square units that cover a region. Have students devise and carry out a plan for finding the area of the classroom. Discuss their results.

◆ **Say:** *We use the formula* A = l x w *to find the area of a rectangle. The solution is always expressed in square units.*

◆ Assign students the appropriate practice page(s) to support their understanding of the skill.

Assess the Skill

Use the following problems to pre-/post-assess students' understanding of the skill.

15 cm

20 cm

Perimeter _____
Area   _____

Perimeter _____
Area   _____

STAAR Mathematics Practice Grade 5 • ©2013 Newmark Learning, LLC

Name _____ **Date** _____

Find the perimeter and area for each rectangle.

❶

Perimeter _____
Area   _____

❷

Perimeter _____
Area   _____

❸

Perimeter _____
Area   _____

❹

Perimeter _____
Area   _____

❺

3 ft

10 ft

Perimeter _____
Area   _____

❻

4 m

4 m

Perimeter _____
Area   _____

❼

12 cm

20 cm

Perimeter _____
Area   _____

❽

8 ft

14 ft

Perimeter _____
Area   _____

 Tell the steps you take to find the area of a rectangle.

Name _____ **Date** _____

Find the perimeter and area for each problem.

1

Perimeter _____ units
Area   _____ square units

2

Perimeter _____
Area   _____

3

2 in.

12 in.

Perimeter _____
Area   _____

4

7 cm

Perimeter _____
Area   _____

5

Perimeter _____
Area   _____

6

Perimeter _____
Area   _____

7 a rectangular patio 20 feet long and 10 feet wide

Perimeter _____
Area   _____

8 a rectangular table 3 meters long and 1 meter wide

Perimeter _____
Area   _____

9 a rectangular swimming pool 100 meters long and 25 meters wide

Perimeter _____
Area   _____

10 a rectangular garden 4 1/2 feet long and 7 1/2 feet wide

Perimeter _____
Area   _____

☆ **Tell the formulas you can use to find the perimeter and area of a rectangle.**

Name _____ Date _____

1 Kiva is using 1-inch square tiles to cover the top of the tray below. How many tiles does he use?

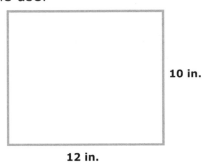

10 in.

12 in.

2 What is the area of the figure below in square meters?

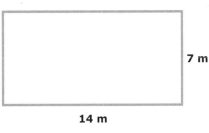

7 m

14 m

3 Mr. Sher's bathroom has the following floor plan. How many square feet of floor tile will Mr. Sher need to recover the floor?

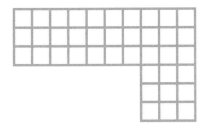

4 If Mr. Sher puts a 1-inch border along the wall surrounding the entire floor, How many tiles will he need?

Circle the letter for the correct answer.

5 The diagram below shows the number of congruent sections in a driveway. The length and width of one section are labeled in feet.

3 ft

3 ft

What is the total area of the driveway?

A 300 square feet

B 900 square feet

C 120 square feet

D 360 square feet

6 Liza's closet floor needs to be carpeted. How many square feet of carpet would she need to cover the floor?

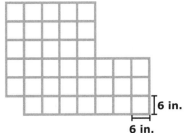

6 in.

6 in.

A 36 square feet

B 37 square feet

C 19 square feet

D 9.5 square feet

Unit 26 Mini-Lesson ★
Find Volume

Standard

Measurement

5.10B, 5.10C Connect models for perimeter, area, and volume with their respective formulas; select and use appropriate units and formulas to measure length, perimeter, area, and volume.

Model the Skill

Draw the following problem on the board.

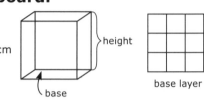

height: 3 cm

◆ **Say:** *Today we are going to find the volume of rectangular prisms by using a formula.* Have students look at the problem and identify the rectangular prism, the height, and the base.

◆ **Ask:** *If we use centimeter cubes, how many cubes form the bottom layer of this prism?* (9) Tell students that the bottom layer is called the base. **Ask:** *If I want to find the area of the base, what should I do?* (multiply length times width) Remind students that area tells the number of square units, and that it is not until they multiply by height (the third dimension) that they find cubic units of volume.

◆ Allow students to use cm cubes to model the problems, proving that the area of the base times the height yields the same answer as counting cubes and layers. Then assign students the appropriate practice page(s) to support their understanding of the skill.

Assess the Skill

Use the following problems to pre-/post-assess students' understanding of the skill.

◆ Ask students to use formulas to find the volume of the following solids.

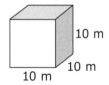
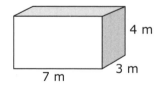
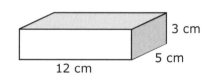

Name _____ **Date** _____

Use a formula to find volume. Show your work.

Formulas for Volume of a Rectangular Prism	
Volume = base (area of) x height	$V = b \times h$
Volume = length x width x height	$V = l \times w \times h$

Remember: You can multiply in any order.

❶ length _____ width _____ height _____

area of base _____

volume _____

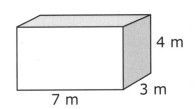
3 cm
5 cm
12 cm

❷ length _____ width _____ height _____

area of base _____

volume _____

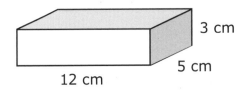
5 ft
4 ft   2 ft

❸ length _____ width _____ height _____

area of base _____

volume _____

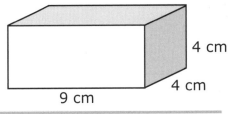
4 m
7 m   3 m

❹ length _____ width _____ height _____

area of base _____

volume _____

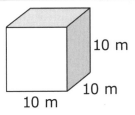
4 cm
4 cm
9 cm

❺ length _____ width _____ height _____

area of base _____

volume _____

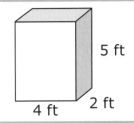
10 m
10 m
10 m

❻ length _____ width _____ height _____

area of base _____

volume _____

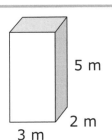
5 m
3 m   2 m

 Tell how you found the volume.

Name _____ **Date** _____

Find the missing dimension. Use the formula V = l x w x h.

1 $V = \underline{\quad} \times \underline{\quad} \times \underline{\quad}$

$V = \underline{\quad} \times \underline{\quad}$

$V = \underline{\quad}$

$V = ?$

4 cm
4 cm
5 cm

2 $V = \underline{\quad} \times \underline{\quad} \times \underline{\quad}$

$V = \underline{\quad} \times \underline{\quad}$

$V = \underline{\quad}$

$V = ?$

4 ft
10 ft   5 ft

3 $96 = \underline{\quad} \times \underline{\quad} \times h$

$96 = \underline{\quad} \times h$

$h = 96 \div \underline{\quad}$

$h = \underline{\quad}$

$V = 96$ cu m

h = ?
8 m   4 m

4 $56 = \underline{\quad} \times \underline{\quad} \times h$

$56 = \underline{\quad} \times h$

$h = 56 \div \underline{\quad}$

$h = \underline{\quad}$

$V = 56$ cu cm

h = ?
7 cm   4 cm

5 $125 = \underline{\quad} \times w \times \underline{\quad}$

$125 = \underline{\quad} \times w$

$w = 125 \div \underline{\quad}$

$w = \underline{\quad}$

$V = 125$ cu cm

5 cm
5 cm   w = ?

6 $180 = \underline{\quad} \times w \times \underline{\quad}$

$180 = \underline{\quad} \times w$

$w = 180 \div \underline{\quad}$

$w = \underline{\quad}$

$V = 180$ cu in

5 in
12 in   w = ?

7 $72 = l \times \underline{\quad} \times \underline{\quad}$

$72 = l \times \underline{\quad}$

$l = \underline{\quad} \div \underline{\quad}$

$l = \underline{\quad}$

$V = 72$ cu cm

8 cm
3 cm
l = ?

8 $320 = l \times \underline{\quad} \times \underline{\quad}$

$320 = l \times \underline{\quad}$

$l = \underline{\quad} \div \underline{\quad}$

$l = \underline{\quad}$

$V = 320$ cu cm

10 cm
4 cm
l = ?

9 $360 = \underline{\quad} \times w \times \underline{\quad}$

$360 = \underline{\quad} \times w$

$w = 360 \div \underline{\quad}$

$w = \underline{\quad}$

$V = 360$ cu units

9 units
10 units   n units

10 $80 = 4 \times \underline{\quad} \times h$

$80 = \underline{\quad} \times h$

$h = 80 \div \underline{\quad}$

$h = \underline{\quad}$

$V = 80$ cu cm

h = ?
4 cm
4 cm

 Tell how you solved the problem.

    STAAR Mathematics Practice Grade 5 • ©2013 Newmark Learning, LLC

Name _____ **Date** _____

Solve each problem. Show your work.

1 Matt wants to mail a book that is 8 inches long, 5 inches wide, and 2 inches thick. What is the smallest possible volume of a box that the book will fit in?

2 The area of the base of a box is 9 square units. If the height of the box is 10 units, what is the volume of the box?

3 The refrigerator box is 6 feet tall, 4 feet deep, and 4 feet wide. What is the volume of the box?

4 The gift box is 10 centimeters by 12 centimeters by 3 centimeters. What is the volume of the box?

5 The dimensions of a large pizza box are 16 in x 16 in x 2 in. What is the volume of the box?

6 The base area of the suitcase is 308 square inches. If the height of the suitcase is 9 inches, what is the volume of the suitcase?

Circle the letter for the correct answer.

7 What is the volume of this rectangular prism?

$V = ?$

16 cm, 4 cm, 4 cm

A 64 sq cm
B 128 sq cm
C 256 sq cm
D 256 cu cm

8 The volume of a cube-shaped box is 27 cubic centimeters. What is the height of the box?

A 7 cm
B 8 cm
C 9 cm
D 3 cm

Unit 27 Mini-Lesson ★

Solve Problems with Temperature and Time

Standard	**Measurement**

Measurement

5.11A (SS) Solve problems involving changes in temperature.

5.11B (SS) Solve problems involving elapsed time.

5.14C Select or develop an appropriate problem-solving plan or strategy, including drawing a picture, looking for a pattern, systematic guessing and checking, acting it out, making a table, working a simpler problem, or working backwards to solve a problem.

Model the Skill

Write the following problem on the board.

At 11:00 P.M. the temperature was 15ºF. The temperature dropped 4 degrees an hour until 3:00 A.M. What was the temperature at 3:00 A.M.?

◆ **Ask:** *What strategies can we use to solve this problem?* (draw a picture, make a table) Discuss and try students' plans.

◆ **Say:** *We can break the problem into two parts, an elapsed time part and a temperature part.* **Ask:** *How many hours are there between 11 and 3?* (4) Draw a clock and shade in the section from 11 to 3. Count the hours.

◆ **Say:** *So the temperature dropped 4 degrees each hour for 4 hours.* **Ask:** *How can we find the temperature after 4 hours?* Draw a number line or a thermometer. Mark the temperature at 11 P.M. and then make hops of 4 degrees backwards for each hour. Have students read the result. (minus 1 or 1 below 0)

◆ Assign students the appropriate practice page(s) to support their understanding of the skill.

Assess the Skill

Use the following problems to pre-/post-assess students' understanding of the skill.

What is the time 5 hours later?

What is the time 4 hours earlier?

What is the time 2 1/2 hours later?

If the temperature drops 5 degrees, what is the temperature?

If the temperature rises 16 degrees, what is the temperature?

STAAR Mathematics Practice Grade 5 • ©2013 Newmark Learning, LLC

Name _____ Date _____

The temperature rises 7 degrees, then falls 12 degrees at night.

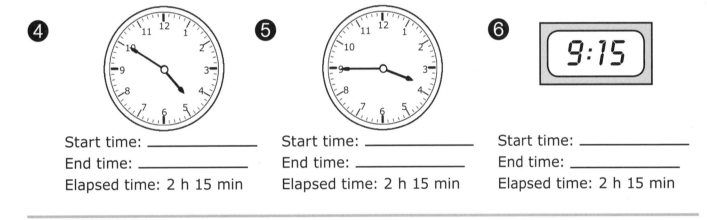

1

Temperature shown is _____
Temperature rises to _____
Night temperature is _____

2

Temperature shown is _____
Temperature rises to _____
Night temperature is _____

The clocks show start times for bus tours of the city.

4

Start time: _____
End time: _____
Elapsed time: 2 h 15 min

5

Start time: _____
End time: _____
Elapsed time: 2 h 15 min

6

Start time: _____
End time: _____
Elapsed time: 2 h 15 min

7 In the morning, the temperature was 15°F. It rose 26 degrees for the high of the day. What was the day's high temperature?

8 One cold night the temperature fell from 27°F to 12°F. How many degrees did the temperature fall?

9 A bus left school at 9:27 A.M. It took 75 minutes to reach the museum. What time was it when the bus arrived at the museum?

☆ **Tell how you found the night temperature for Problems 1 and 2.**

Name _____ **Date** _____

Solve.

❶

An increase of 9 degrees is _____ °F

❷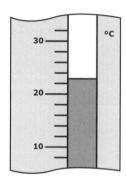

An increase of 15 degrees is _____ °C

❸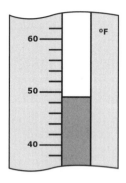

Elapsed time is _____

❹

Elapsed time is _____

Bus Schedule					
Bus	**Depart**	**Arrive Stop 1**	**Arrive Stop 2**	**Arrive Stop 3**	**Arrive Stop 4**
A	7:20 A.M.	7:35 A.M.	7:57 A.M.	8:20 A.M.	7:45 A.M.
B	7:47 A.M.	8:02 A.M.	8:25 A.M.	9:05 A.M.	9:30 A.M.

❺ Use the schedule above. If you miss bus A, how long do you wait for bus B?

_____

❻ If you take bus A at 7:20 A.M. to its last stop, how long does the trip take?

_____

The temperature rises 11 degrees, then falls 19 degrees at night.

❼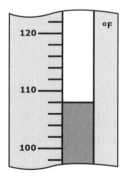

Temperature shown is _____
Temperature rises to _____
Night temperature is _____

❽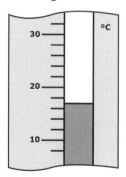

Temperature shown is _____
Temperature rises to _____
Night temperature is _____

⭐ **Tell how you used the bus schedule to find elapsed time for Problems 7 and 8.**

Name _____ **Date** _____

Solve.

1 A one-hour-long television show has 6 commercial breaks of a minute and a half each. How much of the show is *not* commercials?

2 Jane began walking to school at 8:07 A.M. She stopped to talk to the crossing guard for 2 minutes. She finally arrived at school at 8:24. How much of that time did Jane spend actually walking?

3 Carmen rode her bike to the tetherball courts at 4:02 P.M. She arrived at 4:15 and played tetherball for 38 minutes and then rode her bike home in a record-breaking 11 minutes. What time did she get home?

4 Harrison caught the 5:48 bus home from football practice on Tuesday. The bus dropped him at his corner at 6:06. How long was the bus ride on Tuesday?

5 Brenda baked cupcakes on Saturday. The batter took 7 minutes to prepare, 2 minutes to pour into the tins, and exactly 22 minutes to bake. If she started mixing the batter at 11:29 A.M., what time was the first batch ready?

6 The low temperature on Tuesday was 69°F. The temperature rose 14 degrees to the high in the afternoon. What was the temperature then?

Circle the letter for the correct answer.

7 The temperature in the morning was 59°F. In the afternoon it was 17 degrees higher. The temperature fell 23 degrees in the evening. What was the temperature then?

    A 36°F
    B 40°F
    C 46°F
    D 53°F

8 Adrian is preheating his oven to 350°F. If the temperature in his oven increases steadily by twenty degrees every minute, how much time would it take the oven to get from 210°F to the correct temperature?

    A 140°F
    B 5 minutes
    C 6 minutes
    D 7 minutes

Unit 28 Mini-Lesson ★
Conduct Probability Experiments

Standard

Probability and Statistics

5.12A (SS) Use fractions to describe the results of an experiment.

5.12C (SS) List all possible outcomes of a probability experiment such as tossing a coin.

Model the Skill

Draw a spinner on the board.

◆ **Ask:** *If we spin this spinner, is it more likely the spinner will stop at 2 or 5?* (It is equally likely.) *How likely is it that it will stop on 6?* (impossible) Point out that the probability of an event is always a number from 0 to 1. The less likely an event is, the closer its probability is to 0.

◆ **Ask:** *If I spin the spinner once, what are the possible outcomes?* (1, 2, 3, 4, 5) *How many possible outcomes are there?* (5)

◆ **Say:** *We can write probability as a fraction: P = number of favorable outcomes/number of possible outcomes.* Write 5 as the denominator. **Ask:** *What is the probability of the spinner stopping on 3?* (1/5) Have students explain their reasoning. Continue using the spinner to find the probability for its stopping on a whole number less than 6, less than 5, more than 2, etc.

◆ Assign students the appropriate practice page(s) to support their understanding of the skill.

Assess the Skill

Use the following problems to pre-/post-assess students' understanding of the skill.

List all possible outcomes for rolling a number on a cube whose sides are numbered 1, 2, 3, 4, 5, and 6.

What is the probability of rolling a 3?

What is the probability of rolling an even number?

Name _____ **Date** _____

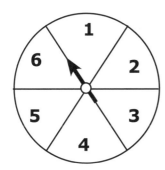

Experiment: Spinning the spinner once

1 All possible outcomes:
1, 2, _____, _____, _____, _____

2 Number of possible outcomes:
_____

3 Probability the spinner stops
on 5: ⬚/⬚

4 Probability the spinner stops
on a number greater than 3: ⬚/⬚

5 Probability the spinner stops
on an odd number: ⬚/⬚

6 Probability the spinner stops
on 7: _____

**Experiment: Picking a letter tile
without looking**

7 All possible outcomes:
_____

8 Number of possible outcomes:
_____

9 Probability of picking Z:
_____

10 Probability of picking a vowel:
_____

11 Probability of picking a consonant:
_____

Experiment: Tossing a coin

12 All possible outcomes: _____

13 Number of possible outcomes:
_____

14 Possibility of tossing heads: _____

 Tell how you found the answer to Problem 10.

Name _____ **Date** _____

List all possible outcomes for each experiment.
Then write each probability as a fraction.

1 All possible outcomes: _____

Experiment: Picking a shape at random

2 Probability of picking a trapezoid: □/□

3 Probability of picking a quadrilateral: □/□

4 Probability of picking a polygon: □/□

Experiment: Spinning the spinner once

5 All possible outcomes: _____

6 Number of possible outcomes: _____

7 Probability of spinner stopping on 6: □/□

10 Probability of spinner stopping on a number that contains 1 digit: □/□

8 Probability of spinner stopping on an odd number: □/□

9 Probability of spinner stopping on a prime number: □/□

11 Probability of spinner stopping on a composite number: □/□

 When you show a probability as a fraction, tell what the numerator means.

Name _____ Date _____

Use the spinner to solve Problems 1–7.

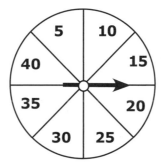

1 What is the number of possible outcomes? _____

2 What are all the possible outcomes? _____

3 Probability of spinner stopping on 6: ▢/▢

4 Probability of spinner stopping on an odd number: ▢/▢

5 Probability of spinner stopping on a prime number: ▢/▢

6 Probability of spinner stopping on a number with a 1 in the tens place: ▢/▢

Circle the letter for the correct answer.

7 What is the probability of the spinner stopping on a multiple of 5?

    A certain

    B improbable

    C $\frac{1}{8}$

    D $\frac{4}{8}$

8 Devon has 1 quarter, 1 nickel, 1 dime, and 1 penny in his pocket. If he takes one coin from his pocket without looking, what is the probability that the value of the coin will be greater than five cents?

    A $\frac{1}{4}$

    B $\frac{2}{4}$

    C $\frac{3}{4}$

    D $\frac{4}{4}$

Unit 29 Mini-Lesson ★
Make Predictions

Standard

Probability and Statistics

5.12B (RS) Use experimental results to make predictions.

5.14A Identify the mathematics in everyday situations.

Model the Skill

Draw the table below on the board.

Results of Selecting a Marble from a Bag and Replacing It 24 Times	
Color of Marble	Number of Marbles
red	10
blue	6
white	8

◆ **Say:** *We are going to use experimental results to make predictions about what will happen in the future. The table shows how many times a red marble was selected at random in 24 trials.* Have students describe the experiment in their own words. Remind students that 24 trials means the experiment was done 24 times.

◆ **Ask:** *Based on the results in the table, how many red marbles will be selected in the next 60 trials?* (25) Help students predict by writing the probability of selecting red, $P = 10/24$ (5/12), and then writing an equivalent fraction with 60 as the denominator.

◆ **Ask:** *How many blue marbles (white marbles) will be selected in the next 60 trials?* (15; 20) Have students explain how they found the answer.

◆ Assign students the appropriate practice page(s) to support their understanding of the skill.

Assess the Skill

Use the following problem to pre-/post-assess students' understanding of the skill.

Softball Batting Practice Results		
Person	**Hits**	**At Bats**
Sofia	4	10
Kayla	5	20
Marti	9	27
Owen	6	18

◆ **Ask:** Based on the data in the table, how many hits do you predict each person will get in the next 36 times at bat?

Name _____ **Date** _____

Use the table for Problems 1–4.

The table shows the results of spinning the spinner 10 times.

1 How many times did the spinner stop on blue? _____

2 How many times did the spinner stop on red? _____

3 Based on the results in the table, predict how many times the spinner will stop on blue in the next 20 tries. _____

4 Predict how many times the spinner will stop on blue in the next 50 tries. _____

10 Trials	
Color	Number of Stops on Color
red	5
blue	3
purple	1
green	1

Use the table for Problems 5–9.

Experiment: A shape is picked at random from a bag, recorded, and replaced. The table shows the results of picking a shape 25 times.

5 How many times was a circle picked? _____

6 Predict how many times a circle will be picked in the next 50 trials. _____

7 How many times was a square picked? _____

8 Predict how many times a square will be picked in the next 50 trials. _____

9 Based on the results in the table, predict how many times a triangle will be picked in the next 100 trials. _____

25 Trials	
Shape	Number of Shapes
triangle	3
circle	10
square	7
hexagon	5

☆ **Tell how you solved Problem 9.**

Name _____ Date _____

Use the table for Problems 1–4.

Mario randomly selects a name from a bag, records it, and puts it back 15 times. The table shows the results.

Raffle Tickets	
Name	Number of Times Selected
April	1
Brett	3
Chase	2
Steve	5
Lida	4

1 Based on the table, predict how many times Brett will be selected in the next 30 tries. _____

2 How many times will Lida be selected in the next 30 tries? _____

3 How many times will April be selected in the next 45 tries? _____

4 If a name is picked more than 10 times, that person wins the grand prize. Predict who the winner might be after the next 30 tries.

Use the table for Problems 5–8.

Alisa rolls a number cube 20 times. The cube has sides numbered 1–6. The table shows the results of her experiment.

20 Trials	
Number	Number of Times Rolled
1	3
2	5
3	4
4	2
5	4
6	2

5 Based on the table, predict how many times 2 will be rolled in the next 40 tries. _____

6 How many times will 4 be rolled in the next 40 tries? _____

7 How many times will an even number be rolled in the next 100 tries? _____

8 Predict how many times a 3 or a 5 will be rolled in the next 75 tries.

 Tell how you make a prediction based on the results of a repeated experiment.

Name _____ Date _____

Use the table for Problems 1–4.

The table shows the results of spinning the spinner 20 times.

1 Based on the results in the table, make a reasonable prediction about how many times 9 will be selected in the next 100 tries. _____

2 How many times will the spinner stop on 1 in the next 100 tries? _____

Number	Number of Stops on Number
1	2
3	3
8	6
9	5
12	4

3 How many times will the spinner stop on a multiple of 3 in the next 40 tries? _____

4 How many times will the spinner stop on a prime number in the next 60 tries?

Circle the letter for the correct answer.

5 Emma has a bag containing different colored beads. She randomly selects a bead, records the color, and puts it back.

The table shows her results after selecting 28 beads from the bag. Based on these results, which of the following is the most reasonable prediction of the number of silver beads Emma will select in her next 56 tries?

Beads	
Color	Number of Beads
gold	8
silver	5
blue	10
black	5

A 5

B 10

C 28

D 15

Unit 30 Mini-Lesson ★
Make Line Graphs from Tables

Standard

Probability and Statistics

5.13A (SS) Use tables of related number pairs to make line graphs.

Model the Skill

Draw the table on the board next to a grid.

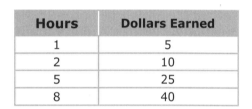

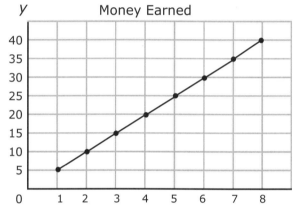

◆ **Say:** *We can use the data in the table to make a line graph.* Give students graph paper and guide them in making the graph shown above.

◆ **Ask:** *What should we put on each axis?* (hours; dollars) *How should we determine the scale on the vertical axis?* Discuss that the vertical scale is in equal increments and must fit.

◆ **Say:** *Now we can plot the points.* **Ask:** *Where should we place the first point?* (at 1 across and 5 up) Plot all the points in the table and connect the points with a line. Point out that the graph gives information that the table does not.

◆ Remind students about input/output tables in Unit 16. If time allows, you may wish to show them how to graph a simple table like $y = 2x$.

◆ Assign students the appropriate practice page(s) to support their understanding of the skill.

Assess the Skill

Use the following problems to pre-/post-assess students' understanding of the skill.

Use the data from the table to make a line graph.

Number of Bagels	Price
2	$1.00
3	$1.50
6	$3.00
7	$3.50

STAAR Mathematics Practice Grade 5 • ©2013 Newmark Learning, LLC

Name _____ Date _____

Use the table to complete the graph. Then answer each question.

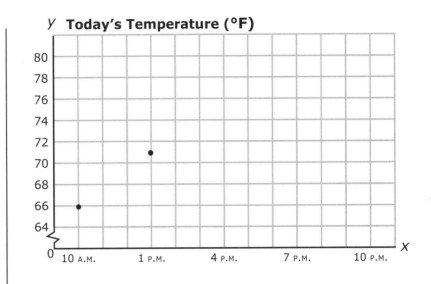

Today's Temperature	
Time	Temperature (°F)
10:00 A.M.	66
1:00 P.M.	71
4:00 P.M.	78
7:00 P.M.	76
10:00 P.M.	74

1 What information does the vertical (y) axis show? _____
Label the y axis.

2 What information does the horizontal (x) axis show? _____
Label the x axis.

3 What was the temperature at 1:00 P.M.? _____

4 What was the high temperature of the day? _____

5 What was the temperature change between 10:00 A.M. and 4:00 P.M.? _____

6 How far did the temperature fall between 7:00 P.M. and 10:00 P.M.? _____

7 When the temperature is over 76°F, fans are turned on in the greenhouse.
About how many hours were the fans on today? _____

 Tell how you used the table or graph to answer questions 4 and 5.

Name _____ Date _____

Use the table to complete the line graph. Then answer each question.

U.S. Consumption of Beef	
Year	Pounds per Person (rounded to nearest lb.)
1910	49
1930	34
1950	45
1970	80
1990	64
2000	65
2009	58

Source: World Almanac, and Book of Facts 2012

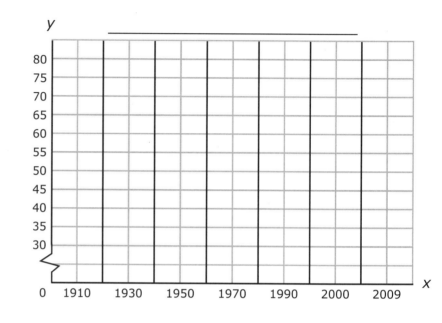

1 What did you do to complete the vertical (*y*) axis? _____

2 What did you do to complete the horizontal (*x*) axis? _____

3 What does the vertical (*y*) axis show? _____

4 What does the horizontal (*x*) axis show? _____

5 In which year did the U.S. consume the greatest amount of beef per person? _____

6 How much did individual beef consumption grow between 1930 and 1970? _____

7 How much did beef consumption decline between 1970 and 2000? _____

8 In which twenty-year period was there the greatest change in beef consumption? _____

 Tell what information you can see more easily on a line graph than a table.

Name 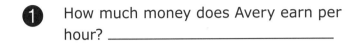 **Date** _____

Use the graph for Problems 1–5.

1 How much money does Avery earn per hour? _____

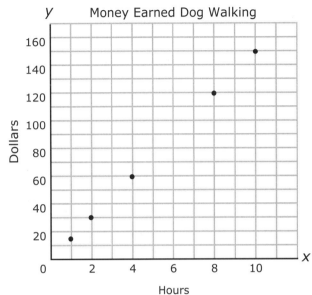

Money Earned Dog Walking

2 How many dollars are represented by each horizontal line along the *y* axis?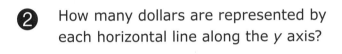

3 How much more money would Avery make if she worked 8 hours instead of 4 hours? _____

4 If Avery worked 7 hours this week walking dogs, how much money would she earn?

Circle the letter for the correct answer.

5 Which table below was used to make the graph?

A

Hours	$ Earned
2	20
4	40
6	60
8	80
10	100

B

Hours	$ Earned
1	15
2	30
4	60
8	120
10	150

C

Hours	$ Earned
2	25
4	50
6	75
8	125
10	150

D

Hours	$ Earned
1	20
2	30
3	40
4	50
8	90

6 Which choice shows the amount of money Avery earns in a year if she works 48 weeks at an average of 6 hours a week?

A $2,880

B $2,160

C $5,760

D $4,320

Unit 31 Mini-Lesson ★
Find Median, Mode, and Range

Standard

Probability and Statistics

5.13B (RS) Describe characteristics of data presented in tables and graphs including median, mode, and range.

Model the Skill

Draw the table on the board.

Class Votes for School Mascot	
Bear	7
Wolf	5
Tiger	8
Penguin	7
Eagle	3

◆ **Say:** *We can describe the data in the table by finding the median, the mode, and the range of the data.*

◆ **Say:** *The median shows us that half the votes are for Penguin and Tiger.* **Ask:** *How do we find the median?* Help students arrange the data from least to greatest and circle the median. Point out that when there are two middle numbers, the median is the average of both numbers.

◆ **Ask:** *What mascot got the least votes?* (Eagle) *The most votes?* (Tiger) Remind students how to find the range of votes. **Say:** *So only 5 votes separated the most popular from the least popular mascot.*

◆ **Ask:** *How do we find the mode of the data?* (find the number that appears most often; 7) Be sure students understand that a data set can have no mode, one mode, or more than one mode.

◆ Assign students the appropriate practice page(s) to support their understanding of the skill.

Assess the Skill

Use the following problems to pre-/post-assess students' understanding of the skill.

Complete. Use the test score data.

Test scores of 9 students: 75, 89, 90, 70, 85, 79, 86, 92, 89

Median _____ Mode _____ Range _____

Name _____ Date _____

Find the median, mode, and range for each set of data.

1

Number of Dog Collars Sold	
May	25
June	18
July	32
August	25
September	30
October	31
November	27

Numbers in order from least to greatest:

_____, _____, _____, _____, _____, _____, _____,

Median _____

Mode _____

Range _____

2

Number of Goldfish Sold, May to November
33, 27, 40, 35, 33, 45, 50

Median _____

Mode _____

Range _____

Use the graph to solve each problem.

3 How many customers were surveyed?
_____

4 What is the median number of dogs owned? _____

5 What is the number of dogs customers most often owned? _____

6 What is the greatest number of dogs owned? _____

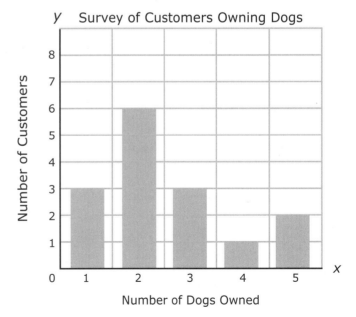

7 What is the range of dogs owned?
_____

 Tell how you used the table or graph to answer questions 4 and 5.

Name _____ **Date** _____

Find the median, mode, and range for each set of data.

1 Median _____

2 Mode _____

3 Range _____

Jake's Math Quiz Scores
87, 79, 82, 90, 79, 95, 85

4 Jake scores 95 on two more quizzes.
How does that change the median, mode, and range?

---

5 Median _____

6 Mode _____

7 Range _____

Number of Students Districtwide in Fifth Grade Classes May to November
23, 27, 24, 25, 23, 22, 22, 25, 25, 22, 21, 24, 24, 21, 25

Use the graph to solve each problem.

8 What was the average sale price in August? _____

9 What is the range of house prices for the months showing?

_____

10 What is the median house price for the months showing?

_____

11 What is the difference between the median and the highest-priced house? _____

12 What is the mode of the data?

_____

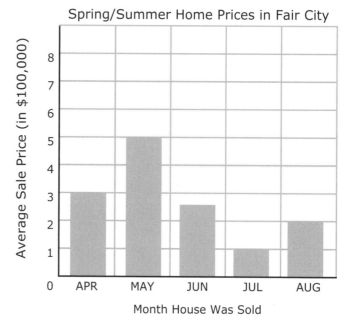

☆ **In Fair City, the median house price for the year is $230,000. What does that tell you about all house prices in Fair City?**

Name _____ **Date** _____

Use the table to solve.

1 What is the range of the data?

2 What is the median of the data?

3 What is the mode of the data?

4 What is the mean of the data?

Amount of Carrots Sold (lb)	
Monday	315
Tuesday	220
Wednesday	132
Thursday	220
Friday	430
Saturday	331
Sunday	128

Circle the letter for the correct answer.

5 The table below shows the points scored in the last 6 football games.

Game	Points Scored
Home 4	24
Away 5	13
Home 6	30
Home 7	17
Away 8	13
Away 9	21

What was the median number of points scored?

A 17

B 19

C 20

D 21

6 Based on the football score data in the table, which statement is NOT true?

A The range of data is 17.

B The data has no mode.

C The median is greater than the mode.

D The number of points scored at Away games was less than the number of points scored at Home games.

Unit 32 Mini-Lesson ★
Graph Data

Standard

Probability and Statistics

5.13C (SS) Graph a given set of data using an appropriate graphical representation such as a picture or line graph.

Model the Skill

◆ **Say:** *We use line graphs, bar graphs, and pictographs to display certain kinds of information. Bar graphs let us compare data easily by looking at the lengths of the bars. Line graphs let us see changes in the data and trends. Pictographs give us a quick picture of data using multiples. The key tells us what each picture represents.*

◆ **Ask:** *Which graph would you choose to display this survey data on favorite flavor of ice cream?* (pictograph) *If many more people were surveyed and 47 chose chocolate and 32 chose coconut, would you use a different graph to display the data? Why or why not?* Give students graph paper and guide them in making a pictograph and a bar graph of the data. Discuss why a line graph would not be appropriate.

Favorite Flavor of Ice Cream	
Ice Cream Flavor	**Number of Students**
chocolate	15
vanilla	10
strawberry	5
coconut	5
mint chip	0

◆ Assign students the appropriate practice page(s) to support their understanding of the skill.

Assess the Skill

Use the following problems to pre-/post-assess students' understanding of the skill.

Make a graph to display the data below. Explain why you chose the graph you did.

Andy's Height Each Year on His Birthday	
Age	**Height (in inches)**
1	29
2	34
3	37
4	41
5	43

STAAR Mathematics Practice Grade 5 • ©2013 Newmark Learning, LLC

Name _____ Date _____

Analyze the data. Choose a bar graph, line graph, or pictograph to display it.

1 Make a graph for the library.

Summer Reading Club	Books Read
Ana	
Ben	
Leo	
Lara	
Jeff	

Each ◯ = _____ books

Summer Reading Club

Name	Books Read
Ana	8
Ben	12
Leo	4
Lara	6
Jeff	10

2 Explain why a pictograph is a good choice for displaying the data.

_____
_____
_____
_____

3 What does the key represent on your graph? How did you decide?

_____
_____
_____
_____

4 Make a graph for a research center on the growth of a new type of popcorn plant.

Popcorn A–3

Week	Height (in inches)
2	1
3	5
4	10
5	24
6	40
7	60

5 Which type of graph did you make? Explain your choice.

_____
_____
_____
_____

6 In which one-week period did the plant grow the most?

_____
_____

 Tell how analyzing the data helps you make a graph.

Name _____ Date _____

Analyze the data and then graph the information.

1 Make a graph for a report on air pollution.

City	Particulate Matter
Chicago, IL	21
New York, NY	18
Los Angeles, CA	29
Tokyo, Japan	35
Beijing, China	80

Source: World Almanac & Book of Facts, 2012

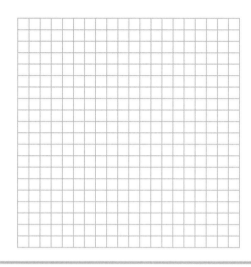

2 The level of particulates is a measure of air quality. The lower the amount of particulate matter in the air, the better the air quality. According to this data, which city shown has the best air quality?

_____

3 What is the range of particulate matter shown in the graph?

_____

4 Make a graph to show the average monthly temperatures in San Antonio, TX.

Average Monthly Temperatures in San Antonio, TX, 2011 (°F)	
JAN	50.5
FEB	55.4
MAR	66.8
APR	75.7
MAY	78.6
JUN	86.2
JUL	87.9
AUG	90.0
SEP	82.9
OCT	71.0
NOV	62.9
DEC	53.4

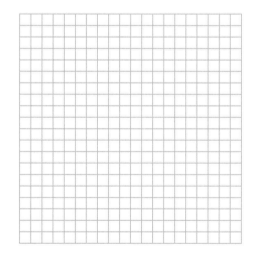

5 Which type of graph did you make? Explain your choice.

_____

_____

6 Between which two consecutive months did the greatest increase in temperature occur?

_____

_____

 Tell how you decided to graph the data in Problems 1 and 4.

Name _____ Date _____

1 What type of graph would best display the data on the right? Explain your reasoning.

_____

_____

_____

_____

Favorite Sport to Play	
Sport	Number of Votes
Baseball	20
Soccer	15
Football	10
Basketball	25

2 Analyze the data below. Then graph the information.

Dog Breed	Average Weight in Pounds
Labrador Retriever	75 lbs
German Shepherd	85 lbs
Yorkshire Terrier	6 lbs
Golden Retriever	70 lbs
Beagle	24 lbs
Boxer	60 lbs
Bulldog	45 lbs

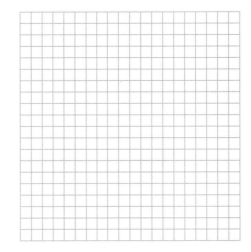

Circle the letter for the correct answer.

3 Which data is best displayed in a line graph?

   A Data on the highest temperatures ever recorded

   B Data on the average daily high temperature in 5 cities

   C Data on changes in temperature from noon to midnight

   D Data on highest noontime temperatures for 4 regions of the United States

4 Which data would best be displayed in a bar graph?

   A Data on the number of each breed of cats at an animal shelter

   B Data on the changing rate of cat adoptions at an animal shelter

   C Data on the fluctuating amount of cat food required at the shelter

   D Data on the average number of cat adoptions over ten years

Grade 5 STAAR Mathematics Practice Assessment 1

Name _____ **Date** _____

Reference Materials

LENGTH

Customary	Metric
1 mile (mi) = 1,760 yards (yd)	1 kilometer (km) = 1,000 meters (m)
1 yard (yd) = 3 feet (ft)	1 meter (m) = 100 centimeters (cm)
1 foot (ft) = 12 inches (in.)	1 centimeter (cm) = 10 millimeters (mm)

VOLUME AND CAPACITY

Customary	Metric
1 gallon (gal) = 4 quarts (qt)	1 liter (L) = 1,000 milliliters (mL)
1 quart (qt) = 2 pints (pt)	
1 pint (pt) = 2 cups (c)	
1 cup (c) = 8 fluid ounces (fl oz)	

WEIGHT AND MASS

Customary	Metric
1 ton (T) = 2,000 pounds (lb)	1 kilogram (kg) = 1,000 grams (g)
1 pound (lb) = 16 ounces (oz)	1 gram (g) = 1,000 milligrams (mg)

TIME

1 year = 12 months
1 year = 52 weeks
1 week = 7 days
1 day = 24 hours
1 hour = 60 minutes
1 minute = 60 seconds

PERIMETER

Square	$P = 4 \times s$
Rectangle	$P = (2 \times l) + (2 \times w)$

AREA

Square	$A = s \times s$
Rectangle	$A = l \times w$

VOLUME

Cube	$V = s \times s \times s$
Rectangular prism	$V = l \times w \times h$

Solve.

1 Elise mowed $2\frac{5}{6}$ lawns yesterday. Which of the following fractions is equivalent to $2\frac{5}{6}$?

A $\frac{12}{6}$

B $\frac{16}{6}$

C $\frac{17}{6}$

D $\frac{18}{6}$

2 Reggie ran $4\frac{3}{5}$ miles training for a race. Which of the following fractions is equivalent to $4\frac{3}{5}$?

A $\frac{20}{5}$

B $\frac{23}{5}$

C $\frac{24}{5}$

D $\frac{25}{5}$

3 Nadia lives $4\frac{7}{8}$ miles away from her school. Which of the following fractions is equivalent to $4\frac{7}{8}$?

A $\frac{39}{8}$

B $\frac{32}{8}$

C $\frac{28}{8}$

D $\frac{25}{8}$

4 Ramona wrote an essay that is $4\frac{5}{6}$ pages long. Which of the following fractions is equivalent to $4\frac{5}{6}$?

A $\frac{19}{6}$

B $\frac{20}{6}$

C $\frac{29}{6}$

D $\frac{34}{6}$

STAAR Mathematics Practice Grade 5 • ©2013 Newmark Learning, LLC

5 Amy has 3.75 pounds of laundry to drop off. Her brother Karl's bag weighs 0.5 pounds more than hers. How many pounds of laundry does Karl have?

    A 2.75 pounds

    B 3.25 pounds

    C 4.25 pounds

    D 4.75 pounds

6 Kim is 5.25 feet tall. She is 0.5 foot taller than her friend Linda. How tall is Linda?

    A 5.75 feet tall

    B 5.70 feet tall

    C 4.75 feet tall

    D 3.75 feet tall

7 Dwayne is 0.25 foot taller than Aaron. Aaron is 5.75 feet tall. How tall is Dwayne?

    A 6.25 feet tall

    B 6.0 feet tall

    C 5.5 feet tall

    D 5.25 feet tall

8 Sinclair lives 4.75 miles from school. His cousin Andrea lives 0.75 mile closer to school. How far from school does Andrea live?

A 5.5 miles

B 5.25 miles

C 4.25 miles

D 4 miles

9 Mike has two kittens. Mork weighs 7.25 pounds. Mindy weighs 1.5 pounds less than Mork does. How much does Mindy weigh?

A 5.75 pounds

B 6.25 pounds

C 6.75 pounds

D 8.75 pounds

10 A movie that is being adapted for television is broken into segments. There are 3 segments that are 15 minutes each, and there are 5 segments that are 20 minutes each. The rest of the time will be reserved for commercials. If, start to finish, the program is 3 hours long, how many minutes of commercials are there?

A 35 minutes

B 45 minutes

C 100 minutes

D 180 minutes

11 Darla is taking a standardized test. It contains three parts that are each 45 minutes long, and 2 parts that are each 25 minutes long. The entire test takes 200 minutes start to finish. How much time is allotted for a mid-test break?

A 5 minutes

B 15 minutes

C 20 minutes

D 30 minutes

12 Beatrice has a gift card to download music. She wants to buy 14 songs that cost $2 each, and 12 songs that cost $3 each. Her gift card is for $50. How much additional money does she need to spend to buy all of those songs?

A $4

B $6

C $8

D $14

13 Robin worked a total of 100 hours in four weeks as a lifeguard. She worked 5 days a week, and worked the same number of hours each day. How many hours did she work each day?

A 4 hours

B 5 hours

C 10 hours

D 20 hours

14 For a reading program, Paula needs to record the hours she spent reading over 5 weeks in the summer. She spent 90 hours reading. She only has time to read 6 days out of the week. If she read the same amount of time each day, how much time did she read each day?

    A 3 hours

    B 5 hours

    C 6 hours

    D 15 hours

15 Jack is a babysitter. He babysat for 100 hours in 8 weeks. He only works 5 days a week, and worked the same amount of time each day. What is the length of time that Jack usually works?

    A 2.5 hours

    B 3 hours

    C 4.5 hours

    D 5 hours

16 Yoko has a collection of 120 snow globes. She uses 4 glass cases to display them. Each glass case has 3 levels. If each level holds the same number of snow globes, how many are on each level?

    A 5 snow globes

    B 8 snow globes

    C 10 snow globes

    D 20 snow globes

17 Roger is moving 60 boxes in his truck. Each box weighs between 28 and 40 pounds. Which of the following is a reasonable estimate of the total weight of the boxes?

A 67,200 pounds

B 2,000 pounds

C 1,320 pounds

D 1,200 pounds

18 Angela makes jams for a living. She has 52 boxes of strawberries. There are approximately 19 to 26 berries per box. Which of the following is a reasonable estimate of the total number of strawberries she has?

A 364 berries

B 800 berries

C 12,000 berries

D 27,000 berries

19 Jimi goes to a record store and buys 33 records. Each record costs between $18 and $23. Which of the following is a reasonable estimate for how much money Jimi spends on records?

A $500

B $1,300

C $875

D $660

20 Quinn is training for a race. She wants to run the same number of miles each week. The table below shows the number of miles she plans to run by the end of certain weeks.

Quinn's Training Plan

Week	Total Miles
1	25
4	100
6	150
9	225

Based on this information, which of the following statements is true?

A The total number of miles she runs will be 20 times the number of weeks.

B The total number of miles she runs will be 25 times the number of weeks.

C The total number of miles she runs will be 20 more than the number of weeks.

D The total number of miles she runs will be 25 more than the number of weeks.

STAAR Mathematics Practice Grade 5 • ©2013 Newmark Learning, LLC

21 Andy is researching for a paper. He wants to read the same number of articles each day. The table below shows the number of articles he plans to have read by the end of various days.

Andy's Research Plan

Day	Total Articles
1	8
4	32
6	48
9	72

Based on this information, which of the following statements is true?

A The number of articles he reads will be 20 times the number of days.

B The number of articles he reads will be 7 more than the number of days.

C The number of articles he reads will be 8 times the number of days.

D The number of articles he reads will be 32 more than the number of days.

22 José has to translate an article from Spanish into English. He wants to translate the same number of sentences each hour. The table below shows the number of sentences he plans to have translated by the end of each hour.

José's Translation Plan

Time, in Hours	Sentences
1	30
4	120
6	180
9	270

Based on this information, which of the following statements is true?

A The number of sentences translated will be 30 times the number of hours.

B The number of sentences translated will be 30 more than the number of hours.

C The number of sentences translated will be 20 times the number of hours.

D The number of sentences translated will be 20 more than the number of hours.

---

23 For a parks service renewal effort, each of 4 city parks will receive 30 new trees. There are 6 gardeners that will plant the same number of trees this week. Which of the following equations can be used to find t, the number of trees each gardener will plant?

A $(30 \div 4) + 6 = t$

B $(30 \times 4) \div 6 = t$

C $(30 \times 4) \times 6 = t$

D $(30 \times 4) + 6 = t$

24 Richard buys 3 dozen eggs. He has a cookie recipe that calls for six eggs in one batch. He wants to make as many batches of the cookies as he can. Which of the following equations can be used to find b, the number of batches he can make with this number of eggs?

A $(12 \times 3) \div 6 = b$

B $(12 \div 3) \times 6 = b$

C $(12 \times 3) \times 6 = b$

D $(12 \div 3) + 6 = b$

25 Three brothers plan to spend $18 each to buy their grandmothers Mother's Day presents. They want to spend the same amount of money on both of their grandmothers. Which of the following equations can be used to find g, the total amount the boys spend on each grandmother?

A $(18 \times 3) \div 6 = g$

B $(18 \div 3) \times 6 = g$

C $(18 \div 3) \div 2 = g$

D $(18 \times 3) \div 2 = g$

26 One face of a cube is 2 centimeters long. What is also true of this cube?

A The volume of the cube is 12 cm³.

B Each face of the cube has an area of 6 cm².

C The cube has a total surface area of 16 cm².

D The volume of the cube is 8 cm³.

27 A three-dimensional figure has 2 parallel faces. Which figure could it be?

A a pentagonal prism

B a square pyramid

C a pentagonal pyramid

D a cone

---

28 Which point on the graph has the coordinates (4, 2)?

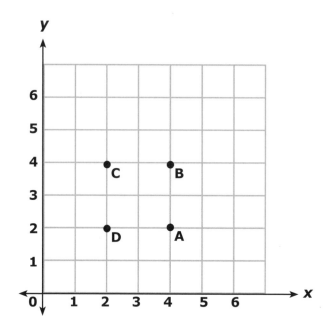

A A

B B

C C

D D

---

29 What are the coordinates of point E?

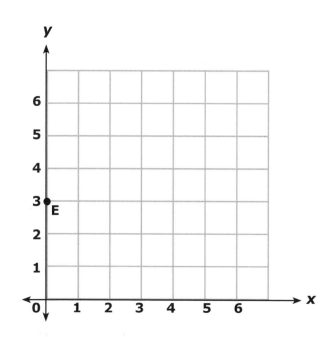

A (3, 1)

B (3, 0)

C (0, 3)

D (1, 3)

STAAR Mathematics Practice Grade 5 • ©2013 Newmark Learning, LLC

30 Which picture shows a rotation?

A

B

C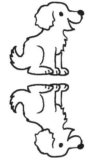

D

31 Which picture shows a single transformation labeled correctly?

A Rotation   **B** Reflection

C Reflection   **D** Rotation

32 Which picture of a transformation shown does not show a rotation?

A

B

C

D

33 Ted wants to buy enough B vitamins for 120 days. He takes two B vitamins daily. Vitamins come in bottles of 80. How many bottles should Ted buy?

A 5 bottles

B 4 bottles

C 3 bottles

D 2 bottles

34 Clare has a water cooler that contains 9 gallons of filtered water. She drinks 6 pints a day from it. In how many days does she drink all the water in the cooler?

A 6 days

B 8 days

C 10 days

D 12 days

35 Chris cooks 2 ounces of oats for his oatmeal every morning. He wants to buy enough oats for 90 days of breakfasts. He buys bags that have one pound of oats in them. How many bags of oats should Chris buy for 90 days?

A 12 bags

B 11 bags

C 10 bags

D 9 bags

36 Mike wants to buy enough cat food to last for 40 days. His cat Petey eats 6 ounces of food twice a day. How many pounds of food should Mike buy for Petey?

A 28 pounds

B 30 pounds

C 34 pounds

D 52 pounds

37 The diagram below shows the number of congruent tiles for the floor of a bathroom. The length and width of one tile are labeled in inches.

What is the total area of the tile floor?

A 2,000 square inches

B 500 square inches

C 1,000 square inches

D 400 square inches

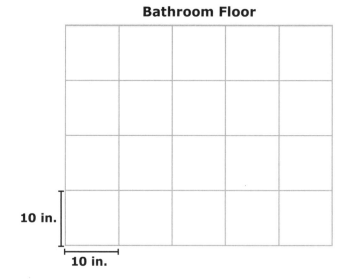

Bathroom Floor

10 in.

10 in.

38 The diagram below shows the number of congruent sections of an herb garden plot. The length and width of one of the sections is labeled in inches.

What is the total area of the garden plot?

A 10,500 square inches

B 2,800 square inches

C 800 square inches

D 700 square inches

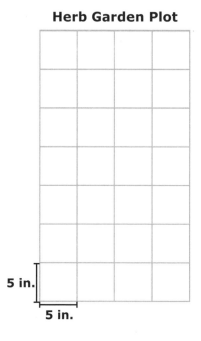

Herb Garden Plot

5 in.

5 in.

STAAR Mathematics Practice Grade 5 • ©2013 Newmark Learning, LLC

39 The diagram below shows the number of congruent sections in a window. The length and width of one of the sections is labeled in inches.

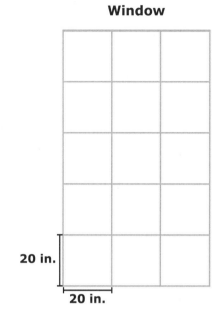

Window

What is the total area of the window?

A 600 square inches

B 1,200 square inches

C 1,800 square inches

D 6,000 square inches

20 in.

20 in.

40 The table below shows the prices of magazines at a newsstand.

Magazine	Price
A	$6.79
B	$4.50
C	$4.99
D	$3.75
E	$8.75
F	$3.75
G	$3.99
H	$7.50
J	$5.99
K	$3.99

What is the mean price of a magazine offered at this newsstand?

A $5.40

B $4.50

C $3.50

D $3.00

41 There is a service that generates advertisements for John's blog. John is testing to see which websites come up. He records the website of the advertiser and refreshes the page 40 times. The table below shows his results.

Website	Frequency
Shoe store	12
Clothing store	6
Tax service	14
Car rental	8

Based on these results, which of the following is the most reasonable prediction of the number of times the advertisement will be the clothing store in the next 100 tries?

A 18

B 24

C 15

D 30

42 A toy prize comes with the kids' meal at a chain restaurant. During his shift, Juan records the toy for the 30 children who order the kids' meal Thursday. The table below shows his results.

Prize	Frequency
Giraffe	9
Elephant	14
Zebra	6
Monkey	11

Based on these results, which of the following is the most reasonable prediction of the number of zebras Juan will see as prizes if 45 kids' meals are ordered on Friday?

A 8

B 12

C 9

D 21

43 Jeffrey hands out yoga mats to people at his gym. The table below shows the colors of the mats he hands out one afternoon. He collects the mats at the end of class, washes them, and then hands them out for the next class.

Color of Mat	Number of Mats
Green	15
Blue	9
Purple	6
Yellow	4
Red	16

Based on these results, which of the following is the most reasonable prediction of the number of red yoga mats he will see in the next class, during which there will be 25 people?

A 8

B 14

C 16

D 26

---

44 There is a website that generates fortunes like a fortune cookie. Erin is testing to see the responses. She records how often different responses come up. The table below shows her results.

Response	Frequency
"Your day will improve."	5
"Smile!"	9
"Call your mom."	6
"You have the uncommon gift of common sense."	10

Based on these results, which of the following is the most reasonable prediction of the number of times the fortune will be "Smile!" in the next 40 tries?

A 10

B 11

C 12

D 19

45 Heather has a bag containing different alphabet pieces. She randomly selects a piece, records the letter, and puts it back. The table below shows her results for 25 selections.

Letter	Number of Selections
R	5
Y	7
A	8
N	5

Based on these results, which of the following is the most reasonable prediction of the number of times Heather will select a piece with an R on it in the next 100 tries?

A 25

B 20

C 15

D 10

---

46 The table below shows the amount of points each basketball player scored during the championship game.

Player	Points Earned
Red Team #4	8
Red Team #8	21
Red Team #15	7
Red Team #18	7
Red Team #27	10
Blue Team #2	14
Blue Team #3	17
Blue Team #10	10
Blue Team #12	8
Blue Team #17	7

What was the mode for amount of points earned during the game by a player?

A 7 points

B 10 points

C 12 points

D 14 points

47 The table below shows the number of pages each article in a magazine has.

Article	Number of Pages
Cover Story	5
Feature #1	8
Feature #2	3
Opinion Column	2
Advice Column	2
Feature #3	4
Review of a Book	2
Review of a Film	2

What is the median amount of pages a given article takes up in this magazine?

A 8 pages

B 2.5 pages

C 3 pages

D 2 pages

48 The diagram below shows the number of congruent sections in a game board. The length and width of one of the sections is labeled in centimeters.

Game Board

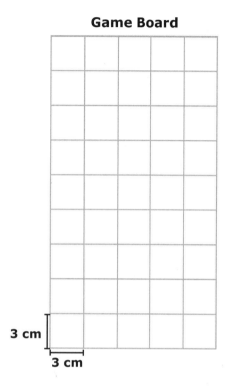

3 cm

3 cm

What is the total area of the game board in square centimeters?

Record your answer and fill in the bubbles.
Be sure to use the correct place value.

			.
⓪	⓪	⓪	
①	①	①	
②	②	②	
③	③	③	
④	④	④	
⑤	⑤	⑤	
⑥	⑥	⑥	
⑦	⑦	⑦	
⑧	⑧	⑧	
⑨	⑨	⑨	

49 The table below shows the number of rooms in each of the houses on one block of Oak Street.

Address of the House	Number of Rooms
145 Oak Street	10
147 Oak Street	9
148 Oak Street	5
149 Oak Street	8
150 Oak Street	8
151 Oak Street	10
152 Oak Street	7
154 Oak Street	6
155 Oak Street	10
156 Oak Street	5

What was the mode for the number of rooms found in a house on this block?

Record your answer and fill in the bubbles.
Be sure to use the correct place value.

			.
⓪	⓪	⓪	
①	①	①	
②	②	②	
③	③	③	
④	④	④	
⑤	⑤	⑤	
⑥	⑥	⑥	
⑦	⑦	⑦	
⑧	⑧	⑧	
⑨	⑨	⑨	

50 The table below shows the number of hours Erica worked each day for two weeks at her temporary office job.

DAY	Number of Hours
Monday	8
Tuesday	10
Wednesday	5
Thursday	8
Friday	8
Monday	8
Tuesday	6
Wednesday	6
Thursday	5
Friday	4

What was the median amount of daily hours Erica worked for this two-week pay period?

Record your answer and fill in the bubbles.
Be sure to use the correct place value.

			.
⓪	⓪	⓪	
①	①	①	
②	②	②	
③	③	③	
④	④	④	
⑤	⑤	⑤	
⑥	⑥	⑥	
⑦	⑦	⑦	
⑧	⑧	⑧	
⑨	⑨	⑨	

Grade 5 STAAR Mathematics Practice Assessment 2

Name _____   **Date** _____

Reference Materials

LENGTH

Customary	Metric
1 mile (mi) = 1,760 yards (yd)	1 kilometer (km) = 1,000 meters (m)
1 yard (yd) = 3 feet (ft)	1 meter (m) = 100 centimeters (cm)
1 foot (ft) = 12 inches (in.)	1 centimeter (cm) = 10 millimeters (mm)

VOLUME AND CAPACITY

Customary	Metric
1 gallon (gal) = 4 quarts (qt)	1 liter (L) = 1,000 milliliters (mL)
1 quart (qt) = 2 pints (pt)	
1 pint (pt) = 2 cups (c)	
1 cup (c) = 8 fluid ounces (fl oz)	

WEIGHT AND MASS

Customary	Metric
1 ton (T) = 2,000 pounds (lb)	1 kilogram (kg) = 1,000 grams (g)
1 pound (lb) = 16 ounces (oz)	1 gram (g) = 1,000 milligrams (mg)

TIME

1 year = 12 months
1 year = 52 weeks
1 week = 7 days
1 day = 24 hours
1 hour = 60 minutes
1 minute = 60 seconds

PERIMETER

Square	$P = 4 \times s$
Rectangle	$P = (2 \times l) + (2 \times w)$

AREA

Square	$A = s \times s$
Rectangle	$A = l \times w$

VOLUME

Cube	$V = s \times s \times s$
Rectangular prism	$V = l \times w \times h$

1 Nigel has a recipe that calls for $3\frac{5}{8}$ cups of flour. Which of the following fractions is equivalent to $3\frac{5}{8}$?

    A $\frac{43}{8}$

    B $\frac{29}{8}$

    C $\frac{24}{8}$

    D $\frac{23}{8}$

2 Sean uses $4\frac{2}{5}$ cans of paint to paint a room. Which of the following fractions is equivalent to $4\frac{2}{5}$?

    A $\frac{22}{5}$

    B $\frac{13}{5}$

    C $\frac{14}{5}$

    D $\frac{20}{5}$

STAAR Mathematics Practice Grade 5 • ©2013 Newmark Learning, LLC

3 Bennett lives $3\frac{3}{5}$ miles from his after-school job. Which of the following

fractions is equivalent to $3\frac{3}{5}$?

    A $\frac{9}{5}$

    B $\frac{15}{5}$

    C $\frac{18}{5}$

    D $\frac{19}{5}$

4 Matt uses $3\frac{5}{6}$ cans of vegetable stock to make soup. Which of the following

fractions is equivalent to $3\frac{5}{6}$?

    A $\frac{33}{6}$

    B $\frac{23}{6}$

    C $\frac{21}{6}$

    D $\frac{19}{6}$

5 Ryan has 9.25 pounds of laundry to do. He fills a bag with 7.5 pounds of the load. How much is not in the laundry bag?

    A 3.75 pounds

    B 2.5 pounds

    C 2.25 pounds

    D 1.75 pounds

6 Sarah picked 4.25 pounds of blueberries. Then she picked 1.25 pounds more. How many pounds of blueberries has she picked?

    A 6.5 pounds

    B 6 pounds

    C 5.5 pounds

    D 5 pounds

7 On Saturday, it snowed 6.25 inches. On Sunday, it snowed 3.75 inches more. What was the total snowfall over those two days?

    A 10.25 inches

    B 10 inches

    C 9.5 inches

    D 9 inches

8 Last Saturday Julia's sunflower was 6.5 feet tall. Between that measurement and this Saturday, the flower grew 2.25 feet taller. How tall is the sunflower now?

    A 4.25 feet tall

    B 6.75 feet tall

    C 7.75 feet tall

    D 8.75 feet tall

9 Ms. Kasey is gathering batteries for the calculators for her math class. She found 12 packs of 8 batteries, and 6 packs of 4 batteries. If she needs 132 batteries for an entire class set of calculators, how many more batteries does Ms. Kasey need?

    A 32 batteries

    B 24 batteries

    C 12 batteries

    D 10 batteries

10 A concert venue has two parking lots. The first parking lot has 3 rows of 14 spaces. The second parking lot has 7 rows of 12 spaces. If there are 100 cars parked in them, how many empty spaces are there?

    A 16 spaces

    B 18 spaces

    C 24 spaces

    D 26 spaces

11 Josh's band played four concerts of 11 songs each and 6 concerts of 13 songs each. Their agreement called for 100 songs. How many extra songs did they play?

A 11 songs

B 22 songs

C 33 songs

D 40 songs

12 Janie needs to print out 8 copies of a paper 12 pages long, and then she also needs to print out 3 copies of a document 15 pages long. She has 125 sheets of paper. How many more sheets of paper does she need in order to print everything?

A 51 sheets

B 45 sheets

C 29 sheets

D 16 sheets

13 Pedro worked a total of 120 hours in 4 weeks volunteering at a hospital. He worked for the same number of days each week. If he worked 10 hours each shift, how many days per week did Pedro work?

A 3 days

B 4 days

C 5 days

D 6 days

14 Kathy is arranging 120 books on 5 bookcases. Each bookcase has 6 shelves. If Kathy wants the same number of books on each shelf, how many books can go on each one?

A 20 books

B 10 books

C 6 books

D 4 books

15 Abe has a gift card to download music. He wants to buy 16 songs that cost $2 each, and 8 songs that cost $3 each. He has a gift card for $50. How much more money does he need to spend in order to buy all of those songs?

A $4

B $6

C $8

D $14

16 Vincent has a collection of 960 baseball cards. He has 4 binders to display them. Each sheet of a binder holds 6 cards. If each binder has the same number of sheets, how many sheets are in each binder?

A 27 sheets

B 32 sheets

C 40 sheets

D 60 sheets

17 Natalie is moving 40 boxes in her truck. Each box weighs between 18 and 23 pounds. Which of the following is a reasonable estimate of the total weight of the boxes?

A 200 pounds

B 675 pounds

C 800 pounds

D 1,000 pounds

18 Rob makes costumes. He has 40 boxes of buttons. There are approximately 27 to 32 buttons per box. Which of the following is a reasonable estimate of the total number of buttons he has?

A 1,200 buttons

B 1,000 buttons

C 12,000 buttons

D 200 buttons

STAAR Mathematics Practice Grade 5 • ©2013 Newmark Learning, LLC

19 Lorrie goes to a bookstore and buys 25 books. Each book costs between $17 and $21. Which of the following is a reasonable estimate for how much money Lorrie spent on books?

A $9,000

B $600

C $500

D $375

20 Seth is training for a race. He wants to run the same number of miles each week. The table below shows the number of miles he plans to have run by the end of several weeks.

Seth's Training Plan

Week	Total Miles
1	30
4	120
6	180
9	270

Based on this information, which of the following statements is true?

A The total number of miles he runs will be 20 times the number of weeks.

B The total number of miles he runs will be 30 times the number of weeks.

C The total number of miles he runs will be 20 more than the number of weeks.

D The total number of miles he runs will be 30 more than the number of weeks.

21 Evan is altering uniforms for the kickball league. He wants to alter the same number of uniforms each day. The table below shows the number of uniforms he plans to have altered by the end of several days.

Evan's Altering Plan

Day	Uniforms
1	8
4	32
6	48
9	72

Based on this information, which of the following statements is true?

A The total number of uniforms he alters will be 8 times the number of days.

B The total number of uniforms he alters will be 16 times the number of days.

C The total number of uniforms he alters will be 8 more than the number of days.

D The total number of uniforms he alters will be 16 more than the number of days.

22 Ola has to edit code for a computer program. She wants to edit the same number of lines of code each hour. The table below shows the number of lines she plans to have edited by the end of each hour.

Ola's Coding

Time in Hours	Total Lines of Code
1	40
2	80
4	160
6	240

Based on this information, which of the following statements is true?

A The total number of lines of code edited will be 20 times the number of hours.

B The total number of lines of code edited will be 20 more than the number of hours.

C The total number of lines of code edited will be 40 times the number of hours.

D The total number of lines of code edited will be 40 more than the number of hours.

23 Kate buys 3 books of stamps. Each book has 24 stamps. She is sending a number of boxes the same size that take 8 stamps to ship. Which of the following equations can be used to find n, the number of boxes Kate will be able to ship?

A $(24 \times 3) \div 8 = n$

B $(24 \div 3) \times 8 = n$

C $(24 \times 3) \times 8 = n$

D $(24 \div 3) + 8 = n$

24 There are 40 tables that each seat 5 guests at a banquet hall for a wedding service. All tables are full. There are 8 waiters that are serving dinner. Which of the following equations can be used to find w, the number of people that each waiter serves during the meal?

A $(40 \div 8) + 5 = w$

B $(40 \div 5) + 8 = w$

C $(40 \times 5) \div 8 = w$

D $(40 \times 8) \div 5 = w$

25 Sandy is planning a book club party. She orders a plate of 35 cookies. There are 8 people in the book club that can eat regular cookies. A ninth person has food allergies, so Sandy requests that 3 of the cookies be gluten-free. Which of the following equations can be used to find c, the number of regular cookies each of the guests without allergies can eat if they eat the same number of cookies?

A $(35 \div 3) \times 8 = c$

B $(35 - 3) \div 8 = c$

C $(35 \times 3) \times 8 = c$

D $(35 \times 3) \div 8 = c$

26 A cube has a volume of 27 in.^{3}. What is also true of this cube?

A The area of each face of the cube is 9 in.^{2}.

B The cube has total surface area of 32 in.^{2}.

C The cube has total surface area of 18 in.^{2}.

D The cube has 9 vertices.

27 Which of the following shapes cannot have all of its faces congruent?

    A a square pyramid

    B a triangular pyramid

    C a cube

    D a rectangular prism

---

28 In the graph below, which point has coordinates (1, 4)?

    A A

    B B

    C C

    D D

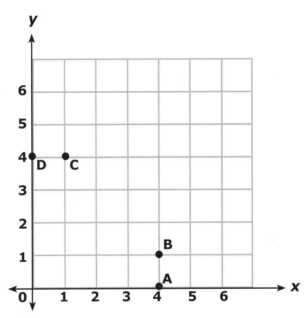

---

29 Which picture shows a single transformation labeled incorrectly?

    A Rotation

    B Reflection

    C Translation

    D Reflection

30 Which of the following describes the transformation?

    A Image D is a reflection of Image E.

    B Image E is a rotation of Image D.

    C Image D is a rotation of Image E.

    D Image E is a translation of Image D.

---

31 Which picture shows a single transformation labeled correctly?

    A Reflection

    B Reflection

    C Reflection

    D Rotation

---

32 Which picture shows a reflection?

    A

    B

    C

    D

33 Kim wants to buy enough C vitamins for her children for 150 days. She has three daughters who each take one vitamin a day. Vitamins come in bottles of 75. How many bottles should Kim buy?

A 6 bottles

B 5 bottles

C 4 bottles

D 3 bottles

34 Steve has a water cooler that contains 20 gallons of filtered water. He drinks 8 pints a day from it. In how many days does he drink all of the water in the cooler?

A 6 days

B 8 days

C 10 days

D 20 days

35 Molly adds 2 ounces of protein powder to her shake every morning. She wants to buy enough powder for 60 days of shakes. She buys protein powder in bottles of 35 ounces. How many bottles of protein powder should Molly buy for 60 days?

A 4 bottles

B 3 bottles

C 2 bottles

D 16 bottles

36 The diagram below shows the number of congruent tiles for one wall of a shower. The length and width of one tile are labeled in inches.

What is the total area of the tile wall?

A 2,625 square inches

B 5,250 square inches

C 2,100 square inches

D 1,050 square inches

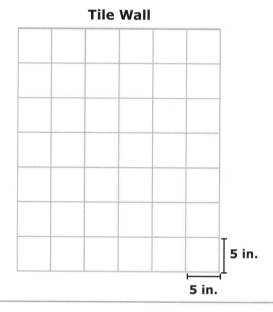

Tile Wall

5 in.

5 in.

37 The diagram below shows the number of congruent sections of an herb garden plot. The length and width of one of the sections is labeled in inches.

What is the total area of the garden plot?

A 600 square inches

B 1,200 square inches

C 2,400 square inches

D 1,400 square inches

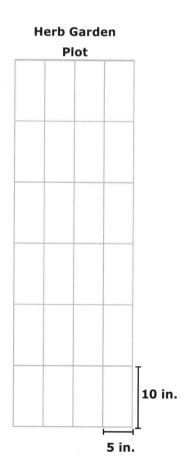

Herb Garden Plot

10 in.

5 in.

38 The diagram below shows the number of congruent sections in a window. The length and width of one of the sections is labeled in inches.

What is the total area of the window?

A 210 square inches

B 21,000 square inches

C 2,100 square inches

D 1,800 square inches

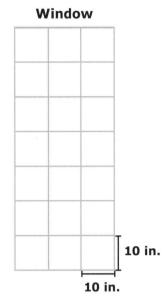

Window

10 in.

10 in.

39 The diagram below shows the number of congruent sections in a game board. The length and width of one of the sections is labeled in centimeters.

What is the total area of the game board?

A 80 square centimeters

B 160 square centimeters

C 320 square centimeters

D 640 square centimeters

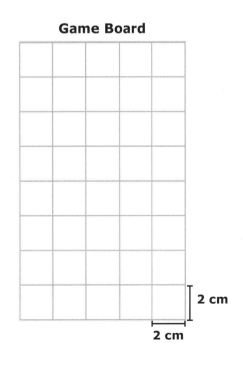

Game Board

2 cm

2 cm

40 There is a service that generates advertisements for John's blog. John is testing to see which websites come up. He records the website of the advertiser and refreshes the page 50 times. The table below shows his results.

Advertisements on John's Blog

Website	Frequency
Shoe store	9
Music magazine	15
News site	20
Phone service	6

Based on these results, which of the following is the most reasonable prediction of the number of times the advertisement will be the music magazine in the next 100 tries?

A 12

B 18

C 30

D 40

41 A toy prize comes with the kids' meal at a chain restaurant. During his shift, Juan records the toy for the 25 children who order the kids' meal Thursday. The table below shows his results.

Prizes with Kids' Meals

Prize	Frequency
Giraffe	7
Elephant	9
Zebra	5
Monkey	4

Based on these results, which of the following is the most reasonable prediction of the number of monkeys Juan will see as prizes if there are 50 kids' meals ordered on Friday?

A 8

B 12

C 9

D 14

42 Ty has a bag containing coins. He randomly selects a coin from the bag, records its type, and puts it back. The table below shows his results after selecting 24 coins from the bag.

Coin	Frequency
Penny	8
Nickel	4
Dime	6
Quarter	6

Based on these results, which of the following is the most reasonable prediction of the number of times he will select a dime in the next 48 tries?

A 12

B 16

C 18

D 20

43 Aziz has a bag containing patterned bow ties. He randomly selects a bow tie from the bag, records its pattern, and puts it back. The table below shows his results after selecting 30 bow ties from the bag.

Bow Ties

Pattern	Number of Bow Ties
Polka dot	4
Paisley	16
Striped	8
Argyle	2

Based on these results, which of the following is the most reasonable prediction of the number of times he will select a striped bow tie in the next 60 tries?

A 4

B 16

C 32

D 40

44 Miriam hands out yoga mats to people at the gym. The table below shows the colors of the mats she hands out for one morning's class. She collects the mats at the end of class, washes them, and then hands them out for the next class.

Colors of Yoga Mats

Color of Mat	Number of Mats
Green	14
Blue	10
Purple	12
Yellow	8
Red	6

Based on these results, which of the following is the most reasonable prediction of the number of blue yoga mats she will see in the next class, during which there will be 20 people?

A 4

B 6

C 8

D 10

45 The table below shows the amount of time 10 volunteers donated to a soup kitchen on Saturday.

Volunteer	Hours Donated
J	3
K	4
L	8
M	1
N	5
P	4
Q	2
R	8
S	8
T	2

What was the median amount of time the volunteers donated that Saturday?

A 8 hours

B 5 hours

C 4 hours

D 2 hours

STAAR Mathematics Practice Grade 5 • ©2013 Newmark Learning, LLC

46 The table below shows the distance Wes ran while training for a 5-mile race.

Wes's Training Plan

DAY	Miles
Day 1	3
Day 2	4
Day 3	4
Day 4	6
Day 5	0
Day 6	5
Day 7	5
Day 8	7
Day 9	9
Day 10	3

What was the mean number of miles per day Wes ran during this training period?

A 4.6 miles

B 5.5 miles

C 5 miles

D There are three means: 3, 4, and 5 miles.

---

47 The table below shows the number of students that practiced in classes at a yoga studio Thursday.

Class	Number of Students
7:00 A.M.	7
9:00 A.M.	8
9:30 A.M.	12
11:30 A.M.	9
12:00 P.M.	15
4:00 P.M.	8
4:15 P.M.	7
6:30 P.M.	17
7:00 P.M.	10
8:30 P.M.	7

What was the mean class size for the yoga studio that day?

A 10 students

B 9 students

C 7 students

D There is no mean in this set of numbers.

48 The diagram below shows the number of congruent sections in a window. The length and width of one of the sections is labeled in inches.

Window

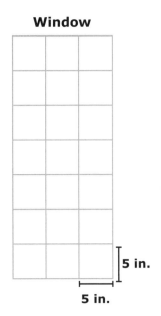

5 in.

5 in.

What is the total area of the window?

Record your answer and fill in the bubbles.
Be sure to use the correct place value.

			.
⓪	⓪	⓪	
①	①	①	
②	②	②	
③	③	③	
④	④	④	
⑤	⑤	⑤	
⑥	⑥	⑥	
⑦	⑦	⑦	
⑧	⑧	⑧	
⑨	⑨	⑨	

49 Amy wants to buy enough fish food to last for 60 days. She sprinkles 1.5 ounces of food twice a day into the bowl. How many pounds of food should Amy buy to last her fish 60 days?

Record your answer and fill in the bubbles.
Be sure to use the correct place value.

			.
⓪	⓪	⓪	
①	①	①	
②	②	②	
③	③	③	
④	④	④	
⑤	⑤	⑤	
⑥	⑥	⑥	
⑦	⑦	⑦	
⑧	⑧	⑧	
⑨	⑨	⑨	

50 The table below shows the ages of the people who work at a certain office.

Person	Age
Person #1	40
Person #2	23
Person #3	53
Person #4	34
Person #5	28
Person #6	36
Person #7	34
Person #8	53
Person #9	29
Person #10	26

What is the median age of the workers at this office?

Record your answer and fill in the bubbles.
Be sure to use the correct place value.

			.
⓪	⓪	⓪	
①	①	①	
②	②	②	
③	③	③	
④	④	④	
⑤	⑤	⑤	
⑥	⑥	⑥	
⑦	⑦	⑦	
⑧	⑧	⑧	
⑨	⑨	⑨	

STAAR Mathematics Practice Grade 5 • ©2013 Newmark Learning, LLC

Answer Key (Units 1–2)

Forest Creek ES
Library

Unit 1 (p. 5)

1. 150,603

2. 1,002,003,000

3. fifteen million three hundred two thousand seven hundred fifty

4. 100,000 + 5,000 + 400 + 6

5. >

6. >

7. <

8. >

9. =

10. <

Unit 1 (p. 6)

1. ten thousand eight hundred seventy-five

2. 100,000 + 5,000 + 200 + 50; one hundred five thousand, two hundred fifty

3. 4,030,957; 4,000,000 + 30,000 + 900 + 50 + 7

4. 10,705,891; ten million seven hundred five thousand eight hundred ninety-one

5.-9. Answers may vary.

10. 81,740<101,978<380,746< 408,083<501,004

Unit 1 (p. 7)

1. ten billion three million four hundred fifty-nine thousand twenty-seven

2. 401,702,368

3. 40,000,000 + 2,000,000 + 60,000 + 800 + 30 + 9

4. 12,111,320 > 9,461,008 > 8,979,554

5. A

6. D

7. D

Unit 2 (p. 9)

1. 20 + 4 + 7/10 + 6/100; twenty-four and seventy-six hundredths

2. 20 + 1 + 3/100 + 5/1,000; twenty-one and thirty-five thousandths

3. 400 + 4/100; four hundred and four-hundredths

4. 100 + 20 + 1 + 6/100; one hundred twenty-one and six-hundredths

5. 305.5; 300 + 5 + 5/10

6. 718.012; 700 + 10 + 8 + 1/100 + 2/1,000

7. 99.83; ninety-nine and eighty-three hundredths

8. 300 + 4/10; three hundred and four-tenths

Unit 2 (p. 10)

1. 6 + 1/10 + 7/100; six and seventeen-hundredths

2. 35.2; thirty-five and two-tenths

3. 4.579; four and five hundred seventy-nine thousandths

4. 802.06; 800 + 2 + 6/100

5. 200 + 6 + 4/100 + 7/1,000; two hundred six and forty-seven thousandths

6. 70 + 4 + 2/10 + 1/100; seventy-four and twenty-one hundredths

7. 8 + 9/100 + 6/1,000; eight and ninety-six thousandths

8. 20.62; 20 + 6/10 + 2/100

9. 95.4; 90 + 5 + 4/10

10. 605.03; six hundred five and three-hundredths

Unit 2 (p. 11)

1. 500 + 10 + 4/10 + 1/1,000

2. 352.4

3. ten and seven-tenths

4. 701.001

5. two hundred fifty-seven and five hundred seventy-two thousandths

6. 900 + 1 + 7/100 + 5/1,000

7. C

8. D

Answer Key (Units 3–5)

Unit 3 (p. 13)
1. <   2. >
3. <   4. >
5. <   6. =
7. <   8. <
9. >   10. <

Unit 3 (p. 14)
1. >   2. <
3. <   4. <
5. <   6. =
7. <   8. >
9. <   10. <
11. >   12. >
13. <   14. >
15. =   16. >
17. >   18. >
19. >   20. <

Unit 3 (p. 15)
1. Answers may vary.
2. Answers may vary.
3. Answers may vary.
4. Answers may vary.
5. Alicia
6. cheddar
7. D
8. C

Unit 4 (p. 17)
1. 11,120,058
2. 974,050
3. 21,141
4. 12,925
5. 1,651
6. 1,009,550
7. 18,213
8. 14,375
9. 438
10. 7,752
11. 10,244
12. 6,795

Unit 4 (p. 18)
1. 23,969   2. 1,022,191
3. 896,711   4. 20,806
5. 65,110   6. 322,541
7. 1,390   8. 37,918
9. 8,808   10. 39,973
11. 1,355   12. 44,878
13. 5,791   14. 52,990
15. 1,175   16. 25,199
17. 6,947   18. 33,431
19. 937   20. 43,410
21. 2,841   22. 14,401

Unit 4 (p. 19)
1. 850
2. $355
3. 4,292
4. $1,990
5. C
6. D

Unit 5 (p. 21)
1. 0.88   2. 0.79
3. 8.77   4. 1.02
5. 0.8   6. 1.12
7. 1.05   8. 1.28
9. 0.14   10. 0.59
11. 3.88   12. 2.91
13. 2.29   14. 8.45

Unit 5 (p. 22)
1. 2.08   2. 1.88
3. 5.17   4. 40.32
5. 25.56   6. 3.16
7. 3.72   8. 40.61
9. 3.9   10. 13.9
11. 6.91   12. 6.96
13. 7.68   14. 12.7
15. 0.66   16. 3.2
17. 6.8   18. 11.11

19. 6.67   20. 2.04
21. 9.55   22. 12.82
23. 0.38   24. 470.49

Unit 5 (p. 23)
1. 14.82   2. 0.98
3. $1.01   4. $1.25
5. 15.12 pounds
6. 0.63 feet
7. A
8. D

STAAR Mathematics Practice Grade 5 • ©2013 Newmark Learning, LLC

Answer Key (Units 6–8)

Unit 6 (p. 25)
1. 9, 12; 1, 3; 9, 12
2. 10, 15, 20; 1, 5; 10, 15, 20
3. 0, 7, 14, 21, 28; 1, 7; 0, 7, 14, 21, 28
4. 0, 10, 20, 30, 40; 1, 2, 5, 10; 0, 10, 20, 30, 40

Unit 6 (p. 26)
1. 1, 2, 4; 8, 12, 16, 20, 24, 28
2. 1, 2, 3, 6; 12, 18, 24, 30, 36, 42
3. 1, 2; 2, 4, 6, 8, 10, 12
4. 1, 5; 5, 10, 15, 20, 25, 30
5. 1, 3, 9; 9, 18, 27, 36, 45, 54

Unit 6 (p. 27)
1. 2
2. 8
3. 0, 6, 12, 18, 24
4. 0
5. B
6. D

Unit 7 (p. 29)
1. 800	2. 1,188
3. 372	4. 1,500
5. 2,793	6. 5,550
7. 13,120	8. 12,798
9. 23,370	10. 12,782
11. 20,928	12. 38,050
13. 34,701	

Unit 7 (p. 30)
1. 2,968	2. 2,720
3. 1,400	4. 4,320
5. 1,168	6. 1,650
7. 931	8. 2,376
9. 6,058	10. 27,590
11. 2,233	12. 15,980
13. 13,146	14. 11,900
15. 18,383	16. 9,984
17. 16,191	18. 14,314
19. 7,843	20. 8,436
21. 10,080	22. 10,530
23. 7,347	24. 34,003

Unit 7 (p. 31)
1. $648
2. 624 miles
3. 33,998 sq meters
4. 10,725 toys
5. 17,856 pages
6. 471,600 meters
7. A
8. B

Unit 8 (p. 33)
1. 242
2. 13
3. 21
4. 27
5. 63
6. 163
7. 181
8. 297
9. 1,618 R1
10. 2,738

Unit 8 (p. 34)
1. 120 R4	2. 67
3. 4,491	4. 27
5. 122 R1	6. 89
7. 21 R3	8. 1,541
9. 405 R1	10. 142 R1
11. 25 R1	12. 257
13. 163	14. 154
15. 114 R2	16. 59
17. 101 R4	18. 251 R1
19. 81 R4	20. 118 R2
21. 938 R5	22. 883
23. 1,456 R5	24. 1,266

Unit 8 (p. 35)
1. 131
2. 12 containers
3. 96 meters
4. 320 gallons
5. 345 miles
6. 586 tickets
7. B
8. C

Answer Key (Units 9–11)

Unit 9 (p. 37)
1. 29   2. 6
3. 22   4. 8
5. 22   6. 25
7. 113   8. 17
9. 30   10. 214
11. 71   12. 15
13. 70   14. 26 R27
15. 160 R22
16. 35 R13

Unit 9 (p. 38)
1. 195   2. 100 R6
3. 17   4. 647

5. 37   6. 89
7. 78   8. 25
9. 410   10. 86
11. 33   12. 425
13. 206   14. 200 R33
15. 240   16. 245
17. 108 R28   18. 37 R6
19. 523   20. 95
21. 201   22. 163
23. 131   24. 1,520

Unit 9 (p. 39)
1. 16 seats
2. 31 feet

3. 291 miles per minute
4. 86 feet
5. 465 pounds
6. 128 cubic feet
7. C   8. D

Unit 10 (p. 41)
1. 30,000   2. 10,000
3. 65,000,000
4. 144,000,000
5. 87,000   6. 42,000
7. 9,000   8. 39,000
9. 250,000,000
10. 570,000
11. 600,000   12. 5   13. 6
14. 2   15. 300

Unit 10 (p. 42)
1. 16   2. 8
3. 9   4. 15
5. 7   6. 8
7. 19   8. 30
9. 51   10. 33
11. 190   12. 123
13. $7   14. $8
15. $9   16. $11

Unit 10 (p. 43)
1. $29
2. $48
3. $6
4. 8,000 stamps
5. $22
6. 7 buses
7. A
8. C

Unit 11 (p. 45)
1. 3/10   2. 0.01
3. 5/1000   4. 0.7; 7/10
5. 0.7; 7/10   6. 0.1; 1/10
7. 0.35; 35/100 8. 0.5; 50/100
9. 0.5; 1/2

Unit 11 (p. 46)
1. 0.1; 1/10   2. 0.01; 1/100
3. 0.001; 1/1000 4. 18/100
5. 7/10   6. 4/100
7. 92/100   8. 1/10
9. 50/100 or 1/2
10. 69/100
11. 10 9/1000
12. 75/100 or 3/4
13. 0.3
14. 0.5
15. 0.4

16. 0.005
17. 0.22
18. 0.017
19. 0.06

Unit 11 (p. 47)
1. 25/100 or 1/4
2. 53/100; 0.53
3. 1/5
4. 0.45
5. 65/100 or 13/20
6. 0.015
7. C   8. D

STAAR Mathematics Practice Grade 5 • ©2013 Newmark Learning, LLC

Answer Key (Units 12–15)

Unit 12 (p. 49)
Answers may vary.
1. 2/6   2. 4/6
3. 6/6   4. 2/4
5. 2/8   6. 6/8
7. 1/4   8. 1/2
9. 3/4   10. 1/5
11. 2/5   12. 3/5

Unit 12 (p. 50)
Answers may vary.
1. 4/6   2. 2/8
3. 4/10   4. 1/2
5. 2/2   6. 3/4
7. 1/3   8. 2/4
9. 3/3   10. 3/5
11. 2/3   12. 1/2
13. 1/4   14. 2/6
15. 8/10

Unit 12 (p. 51)
1. 4   2. 3
3. 10   4. 8
5. D   6. D

Unit 13 (p. 53)
1. 5/4   2. 5/3
3. 9/5   4. 11/4
5. 3/2   6. 10/3
7. 1 5/6   8. 2 2/5
9. 2 1/2   10. 1 1/3
11. 2 1/4   12. 4 1/3

Unit 13 (p. 54)
1. 2 1/4   2. 1 1/2
3. 4/3   4. 12/7
5. 17/4   6. 10/3
7. 1 5/6   8. 2 2/5
9. 2 1/2   10. 1 1/3
11. 2 1/4   12. 4 1/3
13. 1 4/8 or 1 1/2   14. 1 1/14
15. 39/8   16. 47/9

Unit 13 (p. 55)
1. 14/3
2. 3 10/12 or 3 5/6
3. 2 3/15 or 2 1/5
4. 8 4/7
5. 7 2/3
6. 49/5
7. C   8. A

Unit 14 (p. 57)
1. 3/4 and 2/4
2. 5/8 and 2/8
3. 4/10 and 1/10
4. 4/6 and 3/6
5. 5/20 and 12/20
6. 1/3 and 1/3
7. >   8. =   9. >   10. >
11. <   12. > 13. <   14. <
15. <   16. <   17. < 18. <
19. =   20. > 21. >

Unit 14 (p. 58)
1. <   2. >   3. >
4. >   5. <   6. <
7. >   8. >   9. <
10. =   11. >   12. >
13. >   14. >   15. <
16. <   17. <   18. <
19. >   20. =   21. >
22. <   23. <   24. >

Unit 14 (p. 59)
1. Gia
2. Tess
3. Hannah
4. 15 minutes
5. 3/4
6. Wednesday
7. C
8. D

Unit 15 (p. 61)
1. 4/3 or 1 1/3   2. 2/4 or 1/2
3. 10/8 or 1 1/4   4. 2/6 or 1/3
5. 5/3 or 1 2/3   6. 5/4 or 1 1/4
7. 0/8 or 0   8. 10/6 or 1 2/3

Unit 15 (p. 62)
1. 2/3   2. 4/3   3. 1/2
4. 1/2   5. 3/7   6. 6/7
7. 0   8. 4/5   9. 2/5
10. 3/10   11. 3/5   12. 2/5

Unit 15 (p. 63)
1. 3/5   2. 9/10
3. 1/4   4. 3/5
5. A   6. A

Answer Key (Units 16–19)

Unit 16 (p. 65)
1. multiply by 4
2. divide by 3
3. subtract 15
4. subtract 6
5. multiply by $1.75
6. multiply by 31

Unit 16 (p. 66)
1. subtract 13
2. add 1, then multiply by 2 or multiply by 2, then add 2
3. divide by 2
4. multiply by 2/3
5. multiply by 1.75, then add 7.50
6. multiply by 18, then subtract (n–1)
7. multiply by 2, then subtract 3
8. add 2, then divide by 2
9. multiply by 3, then add 3
10. multiply by 3

Unit 16 (p. 67)
1. $160
2. $132.00
3. $42.00
4. $7.20
5. D

Unit 17 (p. 69)
1. composite   2. composite
3. composite   4. prime
5. composite   6. prime
7. composite   8. prime

Unit 17 (p. 70)
1. composite   2. prime
3. prime   4. composite
5. prime   6. composite
7. composite   8. composite
9. prime   10. prime
11. composite   12. prime
13. composite   14. composite
15. composite

Unit 17 (p. 71)
1. 9; 1, 2, 3, 5, 7, 11, 13, 17, 19
2. 4; 23, 29, 31, 37
3. prime
4. 41, 43, 47
5. composite
6. 70, 72, 74, 75, 76, 77, 78, 80
7. C   8. B

Unit 18 (p. 73)
1. $18 \div 3 = n$
2. $4 \times 5 = 20$
3. $18 = 3 \times 6$
4. $n \div 5 = 4$
5. $(5 \times 5) + 1 = 26$
6. $393 = 3 \times n$
7. $654 \div n = 218$
8. $n - 6 = 20 - 19$

Unit 18 (p. 74)
1. $8 \times 3 = n$; ($n = 24$)
2. $2 \times 3 = n$; ($n = 6$)
3. $4 \times 6 = 24$
4. $17 - 8 = 9$
5. $4.50 \div 0.05 = 90$
6. $6 \times 5 = 30$
7. $562 \div 30 = 18$
8. $10.00 - 3.62 = 6.38$

Unit 18 (p. 75)
Answers may vary.
1. $3 \times 8 = 24$
2. $32 \div 8 = 4$
3. $48 \div 8 = 6$
4. $18 \div 6 = 3$
5. B   6. C
7. A   8. C

Unit 19 (p. 77)
Check students' work.

Unit 19 (p. 78)
Check students' work.

Unit 19 (p. 79)
1. quadrilateral, parallelogram, rhombus
2. rectangle
3–4. Check students' work.
5. D   6. B

STAAR Mathematics Practice Grade 5 • ©2013 Newmark Learning, LLC

Answer Key (Units 20–23)

Unit 20 (p. 81)

1. 3; 3; 3; 0   2. 3; 2; 3; 1

3. 4; 4; 4; 4

4. 5; 2 pairs or sets; 5; 2

5. 6; square; 3; 8

6. 2; circle; 1; 0

Unit 20 (p. 82)

Answers may vary.

1. C; three-dimensional figure

2. A; no right angles

3. C; no vertices

4. C; no parallel faces

5. B; not a quadrilateral or D; doesn't have acute angles

6. C; two-dimensional figure

Unit 20 (p. 83)

Answers may vary.

1. Same: Both two-dimensional quadrilaterals with at least 1 pair of opposite parallel, congruent sides and 2 sets of congruent angles and no right angles; Different: trapezoid has only 1 set of congruent angles; parallelogram has 2 sets

2. Same: Both two-dimensional shapes with at least 1 right angle and 2 congruent sides; Different: one triangle, one square.

3. Same: Both three-dimensional shapes with at least 1 circular face; Different: cylinder has 2 opposing parallel faces.

4. Same: Both two-dimensional shapes with at least 2 sets of congruent angles and at least 1 set of opposing sides; Different: pentagon has 5 sides and 2 right angles, trapezoid has 4 sides and no right angles.

5. Same: Both are triangular; Different: triangular prism is three-dimensional, triangle is two-dimensional.

6. Same: Both three-dimensional shapes with no opposing parallel faces; Different: one has a square base with 4 triangular sides and the other has a circle base with only 1 side.

7. C   8. A

Unit 21 (p. 85)

1. (1, 1)   2. (3, 11)

3. (7, 9)   4. (3, 6)

5. (8, 2)   6. (6, 3)

7. (9, 7)   8. (11, 3)

9. (2, 8)   10. (13, 12)

Unit 21 (p. 86)

1. (1, 2)   2. (1, 5)

3. (4, 5)   4. (4, 2)

5. (3, 9)   6. (8, 9)

7. (8, 7)   8. (12, 3)

9. (12, 1)   10.(8, 1)

11. (8, 3)   12. (10, 5)

13. square   14. triangle

15. pentagon

Unit 21 (p. 87)

1. (5, 3)

2. (3, 5)

3. (5, 9)

4. U

5. triangle

6. S, T, U, V

7. D   8. B

Unit 22 (p. 89)

Check students' work.

5. rotation

6. translation

Unit 22 (p. 90)

Check students' work.

4. rotation

5. reflection

6. rotation

7. reflection, translation

Unit 22 (p. 91)

1. rotation

2.–4. Check students' work.

5. C

Unit 23 (p. 93)

1. 0.02   2. 1.3

3. 9,000   4. 0.05

5. 4.02   6. 0.007

7. 30,000   8. 10.5

Unit 23 (p. 94)

1. 0.005   2. 0.36

3. 2.85   4. 1.9

5. 0.07   6. 0.305

7. 6,000   8. 807,000

9. 25,500   10. 1.1

11. 0.45   12. 0.01

Unit 23 (p. 95)

1. 150,000 mL

2. 48.567 metric tons

3. 250 boards

4. 17.5 km

5. 9.3 kg

6. 1.45 km

7. D   8. C

Answer Key (Units 24–26)

Unit 24 (p. 97)
1. 3
2. 5
3. 4
4. 6 lbs 4 oz
5. 30,000
6. 64,000
7. 3,000
8. 6,500
9. 1.75 or 1 3/4
10. 2.5 or 2 1/2
11. 64,000
12. 4.0625 or 4 1/16

Unit 24 (p. 98)
Check students' work.

1. 6   2. 1/2
3. 12 1/4   4. 16
5. 4   6. 5
7. 8   8. 100
9. 108   10. 128
11. 53   12. 40

Unit 24 (p. 99)
1. 5 ft
2. 168 ft
3. 10 servings
4. 4 cups
5. 12 presents
6. 3,570 yd
7. B   8. D

Unit 25 (p. 101)
1. $P = 20$ units;
   $A = 21$ square units
2. $P = 20$ units;
   $A = 25$ square units
3. $P = 28$ units;
   $A = 48$ square units
4. $P = 22$ units;
   $A = 24$ square units
5. $P = 26$ feet;
   $A = 30$ square feet
6. $P = 16$ m;
   $A = 16$ m^2
7. $P = 64$ cm;
   $A = 240$ cm^2
8. $P = 44$ feet;
   $A = 112$ square feet

Unit 25 (p. 102)
1. $P = 22$ units;
   $A = 28$ square units
2. $P = 30$ units;
   $A = 54$ square units
3. $P = 28$ inches;
   $A = 24$ square inches
4. $P = 28$ cm;
   $A = 49$ cm^2
5. $P = 36$ units;
   $A = 53$ square units
6. $P = 20$ units;
   $A = 23$ square units
7. $P = 60$ ft;
   $A = 200$ square feet
8. $P = 8$ m;
   $A = 3$ m^2
9. $P = 250$ m;
   $A = 2500$ m^2
10. $P = 24$ feet;
    $A = 33$ 3/4 square feet

Unit 25 (p. 103)
1. 120 tiles
2. 98 square meters
3. 39 square feet
4. 32 tiles
5. D
6. C

Unit 26 (p. 105)
1. 180 cubic cm
2. 40 cubic ft
3. 84 cubic m
4. 144 cubic cm
5. 1,000 cubic m
6. 30 cubic m

Unit 26 (p. 106)
1. 80 cubic cm
2. 200 cubic ft
3. 3 m   4. 2 cm
5. 5 cm   6. 3 in
7. 3 cm   8. 8 cm
9. 4 units   10. 5 cm

Unit 26 (p. 107)
1. 80 cubic in
2. 90 cubic units
3. 96 cubic ft
4. 360 cubic cm
5. 512 cubic in
6. 2,772 cubic in
7. D   8. D

STAAR Mathematics Practice Grade 5 • ©2013 Newmark Learning, LLC

Answer Key (Units 27–29)

Unit 27 (p. 109)
1. 62°F; 69°F; 57°F
2. 15°C; 22°C; 10°C
3. 4:50; 7:05
4. 3:45; 6:00
5. 9:15; 11:30
6. 41°F
7. 15°F
8. 10:42 A.M.

Unit 27 (p. 110)
1. 58°F
2. 38°C
3. 50 minutes
4. 3 hours, 35 minutes
5. 27 minutes
6. 25 minutes
7. 108°F; 119°F; 100°F
8. 17°C; 28°C; 9°C

Unit 27 (p. 111)
1. 51 minutes
2. 15 minutes
3. 5:04 PM
4. 18 minutes
5. 12 noon
6. 83°F
7. D
8. D

Unit 28 (p. 113)
1. 1, 2, 3, 4, 5, 6
2. 6
3. 1/6
4. 3/6 or 1/2
5. 3/6 or 1/2
6. 0
7. A, E, W, X, Z
8. 5
9. 1/5 10. 2/5
11. 3/5
12. heads or tails
13. 2
14. 1/2

Unit 28 (p. 114)
1. triangles, circle, square, rectangle, parallelogram
2. 0/5 or 0
3. 3/5
4. 4/5
5. 1, 2, 3, 4, 5, 6, 7, 8, 9, 10
6. 10
7. 1/10
8. 1/2
9. 5/10 or 1/2
10. 9/10
11. 5/10 or 1/2

Unit 28 (p. 115)
1. 8
2. 5, 10, 15, 20, 25, 30, 35, 40
3. 0/8 or 0
4. 4/8 or 1/2
5. 1/8
6. 2/8 or 1/4
7. A
8. B

Unit 29 (p. 117)
1. 3
2. 5
3. 6
4. 15
5. 10
6. 20
7. 7
8. 14
9. 12

Unit 29 (p. 118)
1. 6
2. 8
3. 3
4. Steve
5. 10
6. 4
7. 45
8. 30

Unit 29 (p. 119)
1. 25
2. 10
3. 24
4. 15
5. B

Answer Key (Units 30–32)

Unit 30 (p. 121)
Check students' work.
1. temperature
2. time
3. 71°F
4. 78°F
5. 12°F
6. 2°F
7. 6 hours

Unit 30 (p. 122)
Check students' work.
1. add label
2. add years and label
3. pounds of beef per person
4. years
5. 1970
6. 46 pounds
7. 15 pounds
8. 1950–1970

Unit 30 (p. 123)
1. $15
2. $10
3. $60 more
4. $105
5. B
6. D

Unit 31 (p. 125)
1. 18, 25, 25, 27, 30, 31, 32; 27; 25; 14
2. 35; 33; 23
3. 5
4. 3
5. 2
6. 5
7. 4

Unit 31 (p. 126)
1. 85
2. 79
3. 16
4. median would become 87, mode would become 95, and range would still be 16
5. 24
6. 25
7. 6
8. $200,000
9. $400,000
10. $250,000
11. $250,000
12. no mode

Unit 31 (p. 127)
1. 302
2. 220
3. 220
4. 254
5. B
6. B

Unit 32 (p. 129)
Check students' work.
6. from week 6 to week 7

Unit 32 (p. 130)
Check students' work.
2. New York
3. 62
6. between February and March

Unit 32 (p. 131)
1.–2. Check students' work.
3. C
4. A

STAAR Mathematics Practice Grade 5 • ©2013 Newmark Learning, LLC

Answer Key (Practice Tests 1 – 2)

STAAR Practice Test 1
pages 132–155

1. C
2. B
3. A
4. C
5. C
6. C
7. B
8. D
9. A
10. A
11. B
12. D
13. B
14. A
15. A
16. C
17. B
18. B
19. D
20. B
21. C
22. A
23. B
24. A
25. D
26. D
27. A
28. A
29. C
30. B
31. A
32. B
33. C
34. D
35. A
36. B
37. A
38. D
39. D
40. A
41. C
42. C
43. A
44. C
45. B
46. A
47. B
48. 405
49. 10
50. 7

STAAR Practice Test 2
pages 157–179

1. B
2. A
3. C
4. B
5. D
6. C
7. B
8. D
9. C
10. D
11. B
12. D
13. A
14. D
15. B
16. C
17. C
18. A
19. C
20. B
21. A
22. C
23. A
24. C
25. B
26. A
27. A
28. C
29. B
30. A
31. C
32. D
33. A
34. D
35. A
36. D
37. B
38. C
39. B
40. C
41. A
42. A
43. B
44. A
45. C
46. A
47. A
48. 525
49. 12
50. 34

STAAR Mathematics Practice Grade 5 • ©2013 Newmark Learning, LLC